Lesbian POETRY

an anthology

ELLY BULKIN (*b.* 1944), editor of *Lesbian Fiction: An Anthology* (Persephone Press), is a founding editor of *Conditions*, a magazine of writing by women with an emphasis on writing by lesbians. She has written about teaching lesbian poetry in *College English*, *Radical Teacher*, and *Women's Studies Newsletter*; about racism and writing in *Sinister Wisdom*; and about heterosexism and women's studies in *Radical Teacher*. Co-editor of *Amazon Poetry: An Anthology of Lesbian Poetry* (1975), she is a member of the Lesbian Caucus of the National Women's Studies Association and the Editorial Board of the Lesbian-Feminist Study Clearinghouse. She had reviewed women's poetry in a number of feminist periodicals. An intermittent college teacher of English and Women's Studies, she worked for five years at the Women's Center of Brooklyn College. A Jewish lesbian whose father and maternal grandparents emigrated from Eastern Europe, she grew up in the Bronx and has lived nearly all of her life in New York City. She now lives in Brooklyn with her lover and their ten-year-old daughter Anna.

JOAN LARKIN (*b.* 1939) is the author of a collection of poems entitled *Housework* (Out & Out Books, 1975). Her work appears in numerous periodicals and anthologies and on the LP recording *A Sign/I Was Not Alone*. She has published reviews in *Ms.*, *Sinister Wisdom*, *Woman Poet*, and other journals, is co-editor of *Amazon Poetry*, and is the recipient of two CAPS grants for poetry (New York State Council on the Arts, 1975, 1979). She is a founding editor of Out & Out Books, a women's independent publishing company which has published several volumes of poetry and prose and a series of pamphlets documenting ideas important in the evolution of lesbian/feminism. She has taught writing since 1969 at Brooklyn College, where she is currently an instructor in the MFA program in poetry. She has taught at the national Women's Writing Workshops at Hartwick College and has organized and taught women's writing workshops in New York, Maine, and Florida. She grew up in five Massachusetts towns near Boston. Of Scottish and Russian/Lithuanian/Jewish ancestry, she dates from childhood her desire for/suspicion of neat labels. For the past thirteen years she has lived with her daughter Kate in Park Slope, Brooklyn. Still learning to live with irresolvable contradictions, she is working on a sense of humor.

Lesbian POETRY

an anthology

edited by:

Elly Bulkin & Joan Larkin

PERSEPHONE PRESS

Watertown, Massachusetts

 Published in the United States by Persephone Press, Inc., Post Office Box 7222, Watertown, Massachusetts 02172.

Cover design by Maria von Brincken.
Text design by Pat McGloin
Typeset by Eileen Brady.

First Edition. First Printing.

Library of Congress Cataloging in Publication Data

Main entry under title:

Lesbian poetry, an anthology.

Bibliography: p.
1. Lesbianism—Poetry. 2. American poetry—Women authors. 3. American poetry—20th century. I. Bulkin, Elly, 1944- . II. Larkin, Joan.
PS595.L46L4 811'.54'080353 81-2607
ISBN 0-930436-08-3 AACR2

Lesbian Poetry: An Anthology is available free to women in prison.

We are grateful to Judith McDaniel for her suggestion that we organize the poetry chronologically in the order of the poets' dates of birth.

Elise Young, first appeared in *Amazon Poetry* (Out & Out Books), reprinted by permission. **WILLYCE KIM**: "A Woman's Tribal Belt," copyright © 1975 by Willyce Kim, first appeared in *Amazon Poetry* (Out & Out Books), reprinted by permission. "Keeping Still, Mountain," copyright © 1980 by Willyce Kim. **ANA KOWALKOWSKA**: "Azteca IV," copyright © 1975 by Ana Kowalkowska, first appeared in *Amazon Poetry* (Out & Out Books), reprinted by permission. **MINNIE BRUCE PRATT**: "Oconeechee Mountain," "Rape," copyright © 1978 by Minnie Bruce Pratt, first appeared in *Women's Studies Newsletter*; "The Sound of One Fork," copyright © 1980 by Minnie Bruce Pratt, first appeared in *Conditions: Six*; "My Mother Loves Women," copyright © 1979 by Minnie Bruce Pratt and "The Segregated Heart," copyright © 1981 by Minnie Bruce Pratt, first appeared in *Feminary*; reprinted by permission. **GLORIA ANZALDÚA**: "Tres Mujeres en el gabinete," copyright © 1978 by Gloria Anzaldúa; translation, copyright © 1978 by Mary Margaret Návar and Nancy Dean; first appeared in *Lady-Unique-Inclination-of-the-Night*; reprinted by permission. **MICHELLE CLIFF**: "Obsolete Geography," copyright © 1980 by Michelle Cliff, from *Claiming an Identity They Taught Me to Despise* (Persephone Press), reprinted by permission. **BARBARA SMITH**: "Theft," copyright © 1980 by Barbara Smith, first appeared in *Chrysalis*, reprinted by permission. **WILMETTE BROWN**: "Bushpaths," copyright © 1977 by Wilmette Brown, first appeared in *Conditions: One*; "Voices from the Diaspora Home," copyright © 1974 by *Black World*, reprinted by permission. **CHERYL CLARKE**: "Palm Reading," copyright © 1977 by *Lady-Unique-Inclination-of-the-Night*, reprinted by permission; "freedom flesh," copyright © 1981 by Cheryl Clarke. **ALICE BLOCH**: "Six Years," copyright © 1978 by Alice Bloch, first appeared in *rara avis*, reprinted by permission. **KAREN BRODINE**: "The Receptionist Is by Definition," from *Poetry from Violence*, copyright © 1976 by Lighthouse Press; "Making the Difference," copyright © 1977 by Karen Brodine, first appeared in *Conditions: Three*; reprinted by permission. **ELLEN MARIE BISSERT**: "Groves II," copyright © 1972 by Ellen Marie Bissert, "farewell," copyright © 1975 by *American Poetry Review*, "A Romance," copyright © 1975 by Ellen Marie Bissert, from *the immaculate conception of the blessed virgin dyke* (13th Moon); "Ode to My True Nature," copyright © 1980 by Ellen Marie Bissert, first appeared in *Beyond Baroque*; reprinted by permission. **ESTHER SILVERMAN**: "South Bronx Girl," copyright © 1981 by Esther Silverman. **BECKY BIRTHA**: untitled poem beginning "At 20, I began to know," copyright © 1979 by Becky Birtha, first appeared in *Conditions: Five*, reprinted by permission. **ALISON COLBERT**: "The White Worm," copyright © 1977 by *Sunbury*, reprinted by permission. **SUSAN E. SAXE**: "Notes from the First Year," copyright © 1976 by Susan E. Saxe, first appeared in *Talk Among the Womenfolk* (Common Woman Press), reprinted by permission. **DOROTHY ALLISON**: "Boston, Massachusetts," copyright © 1980 by Dorothy Allison, first appeared in *Womanews*, reprinted by permission. **OLGA BROUMAS**: "the knife and the bread," "Amazon Twins," "Artemis," "Sometimes, as a Child," "Sleeping Beauty," copyright © 1977 by Olga Broumas, from *Beginning with O* (Yale University Press), reprinted by permission. **LORRAINE SUTTON**: "Your Olive Face," copyright © 1975 by Lorraine Sutton, from *SAYcred LAYdy* (Sunbury), reprinted by permission. **RUTHE D. CANTER**: "The Resemblance," copyright © 1975 by Ruthe D. Canter, first appeared in *Amazon Poetry* (Out & Out Books), reprinted by permission. **JAN CLAUSEN**: "likeness," "Sestina, Winchell's Donut House," "dialectics," copyright © 1979 by Jan Clausen, from *Waking at the Bottom of the Dark* (Long Haul Press), reprinted by permission. **SAPPHIRE**: untitled poem beginning "She hated the rain," and "New York City Tonight," copyright © 1978 by Sapphire, first appeared in *Azalea*, reprinted by permission. **ROBIN BECKER**: "The Landing," copyright © 1975 by *Aphra*, reprinted by permission. **M. F. HERSHMAN** : "Making Love to Alice," copyright © 1975 by Marcie Hershman, first appeared in *Amazon Poetry* (Out & Out Books), reprinted by permission. **WENDY BROOKS WIEBER**: "One, The Other, And," copyright © 1970 by Wendy Brooks Wieber, from *No More Masks!* (Doubleday Anchor), reprinted by permission. **ELEANOR LERMAN**: "The Community of Women Causes and Operation," "Finally I See Your Skin," copyright © 1973 by Eleanor Lerman, from *Armed Love* (Wesleyan University Press), reprinted by permission. **JANE CREIGHTON**: "Ceres in an Open Field," copyright © 1980 by Jane Creighton, from *Ceres in an Open Field* (Out & Out Books), reprinted by permission. **REBECCA GORDON**: "When I Was a Fat Woman," copyright © 1980 by Rebecca Gordon, first appeared in *Conditions: Six*, reprinted by permission. **KITTY TSUI**: "the words of a woman who breathes fire: one," copyright © 1981 by Kitty Tsui. **CHERRÍE MORAGA**: "Like I Am to No One," "You Upset the Whole System of this Place," "For Amber," copyright © 1981

We dedicate this book to women of every race,
of every class,
of every age,
of every physical ability and disability.

We dedicate it to the women poets in every state and in every country who write as lesbians;
to those who write in prison, at their work places, in mental institutions, in their homes;
to those who must publish their poetry anonymously;
to those who have long been out as lesbians and as lesbian writers;
to those who have found in this book the right place to come out publicly.

We dedicate it to the lesbian poets who could not allow us to print their work;
to the silent women who have not yet begun to write;
to all of the women who find something of themselves in it.

We dedicate it to the women we love who make possible our lives and our words;
to our daughters—and to other women's daughters and sons—that they may grow up to understand.

1975/1980

Prefatory Note

The appearance of this book raises the question—what *is* a "lesbian poetry anthology"? Some expect only love poetry; others, a collection of poems specifically about our oppression as lesbians. Instead, we have put together a book of poems that show the scope and intensity of lesbian experience. They were all written by women who define themselves as lesbians. And who have chosen, by publishing their poetry here, to affirm publicly that identity.

With us, they—and their poems—belie a simple sexual definition of lesbianism. Our lives have many sides. The poetry expresses them—growing up, sisterhood, sexuality, family, motherhood, physical disability, work, dying. Myth. Racism. Imprisonment. Old age, war, ritual. For us, this range says something essential about the nature and complexity of our lives.

The poetry also reflects our belief that, while we suffer special oppression as woman-identified women within a patriarchal society, our oppression does not stop there. Our lives are further circumscribed when we do not meet other norms of contemporary American society—when we are not white or able-bodied or young or Christian or middle-class.

For us, putting together this book combines the personal and the political. The poems convey both private joy and pain and humor, and a larger context of racial, economic, and social inequality and struggle. For many of these poets, the two points touch where there is a deep consciousness of the interrelatedness of women's experiences. Our decision to edit this book grew out of our awareness that, as Susan Griffin has written:

> . . . the risks other women take in their writings, casting off the academic shroud over their feelings, naming the unspeakable, moving with courage into new forms and new perceptions, make me able to write what before could not be written. In every sense, we do not work alone.

Elly Bulkin
Joan Larkin

Brooklyn, New York
1975/1981

Contents

Introduction: A Look At Lesbian Poetry

by Elly Bulkin

> *Of those hours,*
> *Who will speak these days,*
> *if not I,*
> *if not you?*
> —Muriel Rukeyser,
> "The Speed of Darkness"

I.

It was easy, a few years ago, to think that lesbian poetry didn't exist. It had, of course, always been there—dusty in rare book libraries, lost in love poems with changed or ambiguous pronouns, absent from the published writing of otherwise acceptable women poets.[1] Yet until fairly recently, we didn't know all this. Those of us who are lesbians seemed to have come from nowhere, from a great blankness with only a few shadowy figures to suggest a history.

We could find Sappho's poetry, all right, but only when preceded by the (male) assurances that "Neither the gossip of scandalmongers nor the scrupulous research of scholars should cause us to forget that [her reputation as a lesbian] is nothing but speculation."[2] We could surmise about Emily Dickinson's life, but until the fifties we were confronted only with a selected number of her published poems and letters.[3] We could stubbornly claim Gertrude Stein and Amy Lowell and H.D. as lesbians—but they hardly constituted a lesbian literary tradition out of which to write or a history from which lesbians, especially lesbians of color or poor or working class lesbians, could draw strength.

The early women's movement in the late sixties and early seventies pulled together, uncovered, and touted a large group of respectable poetic foremothers. But not for lesbians. When commercial publishers decided several years ago that there was money in women's poetry anthologies, two appeared, but without more than token lesbian visibility. The 1973 publication of *No More Masks!* and *Rising Tides* was tremendously important, but it did almost nothing to establish lesbians as significant contributors to women's literature. The problem stemmed not from the lack of lesbian poets in each book, but from the impossibility of identifying them unless they were represented by poems about subjects connected directly and explicitly to lesbian oppression and/or sexuality.

I remember trying to read between the lines of the biographical statements in *No More Masks!* and *Rising Tides* to figure out whether the author of a poem that moved me was a lesbian.[4] What, after all, did it mean when a woman was described as living with her young daughter? Who was the "you" addressed in very personal terms in a poem—a woman or a man? Where was I in these books? Was there a "we" in them?

The editors were of little help. In her long introduction to *No More Masks!* Florence Howe recognized the existence of lesbian poetry—at least *recent* lesbian poetry—but seemed to regard lesbianism as just one more theme women can write about; its political significance—and history—seemed lost. And *Rising Tides* managed to get through 400 pages (and five identifiably lesbian poets) without mentioning the word once (though we do have lesbian Judy Grahn's ironic description of herself as "insane, evil, and devious").[5]

Yet, however weakly, these early anthologies provided impetus toward the discovery of lesbian poetry for many women who lived away from urban and university centers and women's bookstores and who were unaware of and/or without access to women's press publications, readings, and periodicals. I did find in *No More Masks!* a poem by Wendy Wieber, "One, The Other, And," that I read over and over, having no other poems about the awakening that I myself was then experiencing; it begins:

> That sound like the scratch
> scratch of an old recording
> the static and scratch of an
> old recording that tight
> scratch was the sound of her
> hands in her head and that
> contracted scratch was the
> scar of her mouth and her
> eyes

and ends:

> They hadn't known
> for so much frost
> for bone cold fingers
> of the stunning hand
> and stings of the
> ice bee
>
> they hadn't known
> but gathered themselves
> unto one another
> gathered their selves

into such a wholeness
they took
the blue knife
and slit the belly of night
spinning the sun into life . . . .

Experienced and written about by women all over the country, the expansive coming-out process Wieber describes resulted in a flowering of visible lesbian poetry. Included in such subsequent commerical-press anthologies as *We Become New* (1974), its own strength underscored its pivotal role in contemporary women's poetry.[6] A result was the type of critical consciousness about heterosexist assumptions displayed by Louise Bernikow in editing *The World Split Open* (1974). In her selection of women poets writing about loving women way back in the early 1600's, Bernikow begins to fill in the contour of a lesbian literary tradition and explains why the men who have written literary history have chosen to ignore its existence:

> Such men not only see themselves as "the world," they also see themselves as "love." Women who do not love men, and women who do not have sex with men, in the eyes of men, have loveless and sexless lives. Yet, for all obfuscation about it, the truth seems to be that most of these women poets have loved women, sometimes along with loving men. Women have found in other women exactly the same companionship, encouragement, and understanding that they did not find in men. Whether all the woman-to-woman relationships that exist in the lives of these poets were explicitly sexual or not is difficult to know, for taboo was always in the way and evidence that might have told the true nature of those relationships is missing. Yet what matters most is not who did what to whom in what bed, but the direction of emotional attention. Mostly, then, these women turned to women—and understanding that might be the beginning and end of a nonpatriarchal biography.[7]

This is new-found history. So, all except the youngest lesbian poets—or those who started very recently to read and write poetry—have had their work shaped by the simple fact of their having begun to write without knowledge of such history and with little or no hope of support from a women's and/or lesbian writing community. The differences between them are explicable, to a considerable extent, by the absence or the state of the women's movement when they began to write seriously.

The work of lesbian poets who began to write long before the existence of the women's movement must be understood within that context. Poets like May Sarton and May Swenson have long worked in a world of traditional (white bourgeois male) academic values relating to every facet of poetry—its style, its structure, its subject, its audience.

We can sense Sarton's relief (and pain) when in her sixties—and only *after* her parents' deaths—she felt able to come out publicly through the appearance of her 1965 novel, *Mrs. Stevens Hears the Mermaids Singing.*[8] Finding Swenson's poem, "To Confirm a Thing," in a 1975 lesbian anthology, *Amazon Poetry*, we can read it, more than twenty years after it was written, with particular clarity:

> We are Children incorrigible and perverse
> who hold our obstinate seats
> on heaven's carousel
> refusing our earth's assignment[9]

If readers initially had some difficulty understanding these lines, their response is comprehensible given the poem's date of publication, 1954, two years before the first issue of *The Ladder*, the pioneering lesbian magazine. Even *The Ladder* reflects for at least a decade society's negative view of lesbianism (or what was long described in its pages as "deviance").[10] The weakness of the poetry it published before the late sixties seems to have resulted not only from the relative absence of other lesbian poetry but from the understandable reluctance of lesbian poets to appear in an identifiably lesbian periodical, especially during the assorted witch-hunts of the fifties.[11]

Given this context, the obliqueness of Muriel Rukeyser's coming out as a lesbian in her poetry is thoroughly understandable. Though I try to be alert to nuances that can reveal a poet's sexual and affectional preference, I had read through Rukeyser's work without thinking of her possible lesbianism until *after* I had heard that she had agreed to participate in the lesbian poetry reading at the 1978 Modern Language Association convention; when illness forced her withdrawal, she expressed to Judith McDaniel her hope that she would be included the following year, a desire that went unfulfilled because of her chronic ill health (and death in 1980 at the age of sixty-seven). Sending me back to her work, the discovery allowed me to understand for the first time that the opening poems in *The Speed of Darkness* (1971) celebrate coming out.[12] Only my continued ignorance of Rukeyser's lesbianism could support another reading of them.

Using the persona of Orpheus, Rukeyser speaks first in "The Poem as Mask" of having been "split open, unable to speak, in exile from/myself"; and the poem ends: "Now, for the first time, the god lifts his hand,/

the fragments join in me with their own music." A short lyric is followed by "The Transgress":

> . . . in the revelation
> thundering on tabu after the broken
>
> imperative, while the grotesque ancestors fade
> with you breathing beside me through our dream:
>
> bed of forbidden things finally known–

And the book's fourth poem, "The Conjugation of the Paramecium," describes how "when the paramecium/desires/renewal/strength another joy" it "lies down beside/another/paramecium," *like with like*, in a loving exchange that, we have been told in the poem's opening lines, "has nothing/ to do with/propagating."

These few poems exemplify the potential for erroneous (or, at best, incomplete) reading of a writer's work if we are not aware of her lesbianism. "The Poem as Mask" has been–and can be–read as a positive statement of a woman's going beyond "masks" and "myth" to experience herself as an integrated whole. We can either perceive it in this general way–or apply what we know about Rukeyser's life (and about the following poems) and read it as a poem that thematically is very much like Wendy Wieber's "One, The Other, And." We have the further option of deciding whether to consider the "tabu" in "The Transgress" as a complete mystery or "The Conjugation of the Paramecium" as a purely playful extended metaphor without connection to the poet's lesbianism. We need, I think, to look at these poems within the historical framework of lesbian oppression and invisibility. How else to explain the obliqueness and obfuscation in work by a poet of characteristic clarity?

II.

The flowering of lesbian poetry that began slowly in the late sixties and had reached full bloom by the mid-seventies was rooted in the civil rights and anti-war movements, which supported challenging the various racist, imperialistic values of contemporary American society. Many of the lesbians who published their work in the growing number of feminist periodicals and who began the Women's Press Collective and Diana Press viewed themselves as radicals, as well as lesbians and feminists. Before we could find their poems bound in books, we could find them scattered through a newspaper like *off our backs*, whose 1971 headlines capture the general political climate into which this lesbian poetry was born—*Indochina Lives; Angela Davis Needs Defense Funds; Women March on the Pentagon; Underground in America.*

Many lesbian writers found themselves pushed even more firmly out of the American mainstream by the anti-war, radical left politics of the times. Martha Shelley wrote for *Rat,* a radical newspaper in New York City; Judy Greenspan organized in Madison, Wisconsin against the Vietnam War. Others came from a poor or working-class background that seemed ignored or denigrated by a predominantly white, middle-class women's movement; Rita Mae Brown helped establish *The Furies*, a monthly publication (1972-1973) concerned with issues of class, sexism, and racism. Still others, like Willyce Kim and Pat Parker, suffered additional oppression as lesbians of color.

These lesbian poets were outsiders in American society. They felt no stake in its traditions, in its establishments, in its social/political/aesthetic values. Instead they sought to create a tradition that was anti-literary, anti-intellectual, anti-hierarchical. The tone was captured by Judy Grahn, whose "The Common Woman" poems (first published in 1970 in *off our backs*) celebrate the waitress, the mother, the lesbian, the prostitute, the childhood friend:

For all the world we didn't know we held in common
all along,
the common woman is as common as the best of bread
and will rise
and will become strong—I swear it to you

I swear it to you on my own head.
I swear it to you on my common
woman's
head.

Grahn's direct, everyday language with a rhetorical drive draws on oral traditions of poetry—biblical, Black, beat, protesting—and seems meant to be read aloud at women's meetings. This oral quality, the sense that the poem should be heard with others, not read by oneself, is in the ending, too, of Judy Greenspan's "To Lesbians Everywhere":

and someday
there will be a great rumbling
and we will join with all people
charging forth like the wind
they will never know what hit them.[13]

The focus in these and other poems is on the poem as bridge, not as obstacle. The work of these early lesbian writers seems to be deliberately, perhaps even defiantly, "anti-poetic." When they were gathered into books in the early seventies, the poems of these writers stood for a brief while as a separate, identifiable body of lesbian poetry.

Yet, even as these books were being printed, newer poems, appearing with increasing regularity in women's magazines and newspapers, were being written by an ever-widening group of women who defined themselves as lesbians. The reasons for this sudden increase in the number of women poets who so defined themselves are complex, involving changes within individual women, the women's movement, and women's poetry. These interactions—personal, political, poetic—are basic, but different for each woman.

Contemporary lesbian poetry comes from many sources. The earlier lesbian poets—Judy Grahn, Pat Parker, Fran Winant—continue to write. Long established poets like May Sarton and May Swenson have allowed themselves to be identified publicly as lesbians. Lesbian poets like Audre Lorde (published by Diane di Prima's Poets Press in the late sixties and by a small black male press in the early seventies) and Susan Sherman (published by a small white male press in the early seventies) can become more direct in their work and more publicly perceived as *lesbian* activists. Women who had already published heterosexually-identified poetry with large commercial presses and reaped Establishment rewards for it—Marilyn Hacker, Adrienne Rich—write from a lesbian-feminist perspective. A whole range of lesbian poets (most of whom had written earlier heterosexual poetry) put out exciting self-published and women's press books.

III.

The dramatic increase in the number of lesbian poets has also helped provide the impetus for uncovering an historical tradition of lesbian poetry. Much of the work that has been done on the best known lesbian poets—Sappho, Emily Dickinson, H.D., Amy Lowell, Gertrude Stein—has been done by lesbians since the early seventies, contemporaneous with the growth of this poetry. Ongoing current work by Judith McDaniel on white, economically privileged poets who wrote at the beginning of the century—Edna St. Vincent Millay, Sara Teasdale, Elinor Wylie, and others—reveals the tremendous extent to which they fueled each others' poetry and lives; while not necessarily lesbian in the narrowest sense, the community and the poetry they created certainly rests solidly on the "lesbian continuum" of woman-identified experience discussed by Rich in "Compulsory Heterosexuality and Lesbian Existence."[14] Unequivocally lesbian is the life of Angelina Weld Grimké, the Black descendant of slaves and slave-owners, whose unpublished love poetry, diary entries, and letters were unearthed by Gloria T. Hull in her research on women poets of the Harlem Renaissance.[15]

Uncovering a poetic tradition representative of lesbians of color and poor and working-class lesbians of all races involves, as Barbara Noda has written, reexamining "the words 'lesbian,' 'historical,' and even 'poet'." A beginning problem is definitional, as Paula Gunn Allen makes clear in her exploration of her own American Indian culture:

It is not known if those
who warred and hunted on the plains
chanted and hexed in the hills
divined and healed in the mountains
gazed and walked beneath the seas
were Lesbians
It is never known
if any woman was a lesbian

The search is further compounded when the goal is finding not just a lesbian, but a lesbian *poet*, especially among those groups—Latinas, Appalachian women, and others—whose historical poverty leaves them without a tradition of "literacy" (or "literacy" in English), and without a way to get their written or oral poetry reproduced and distributed. We face a particular obstacle in attempting to uncover historical material by/about American Indian lesbians: the obligation to respect the beliefs of those tribes which maintain that the very act of writing down myths and stories is an act of disempowerment.[16]

The near impossibility of doing certain kinds of historical research is illustrated by Noda's response to my question about the feasibility of locating an Asian-American lesbian poetry tradition:

> Perhaps I could ask my 87-year-old grandmother who is one of the still remaining Issei women *if* she remembers any "strange" women who did not marry and associated mainly with other women. *If* by chance she could relate to the question and did remember such a woman, I would then have to trace the whereabouts of the woman. *If* the woman was still alive or not, *if* the woman left any available writings, I would then have a glimmer of a source that is historical rather than contemporary of an Asian-American lesbian. With the Goddess' blessing she would have been a poet and truthfully such a woman would not be considered an Asian-American. Because if she was an Issei like my grandmother, then she had been born in Japan and emigrated to the United States to become the first generation of women to live here.[17]

While the exact situation Noda describes is specific to Asian-Americans as a comparatively recent immigrant group, it also outlines general problems of finding lesbians—let alone lesbian poets.

Even where a lesbian poet is alive and quite ready to tell us that she has always been a lesbian, we need to look carefully at a concept of the "historical" that probably makes us more likely to place within a "lesbian historical tradition" someone like H.D., who was born in 1886 and died in 1961, than someone like Elsa Gidlow who was born in 1898, was writing lesbian love poetry at sixteen, and today continues to write. Gidlow, of course, lacked H.D.'s economic benefits—Bryn Mawr, travel to London, acceptance into the "cultured" world of Ezra Pound and the "Imagists." Instead, Gidlow reminds us to look for part of our tradition in the work and life of a lesbian who was the first born to a large, poor, white family; went without "the grammar school-high school-college education" she "craved"; spent "a lifetime of working fulltime to support . . . [herself] (and others at times)" and wrote both love poetry and "bitter social protest poetry."[18] Gidlow movingly depicts her attempts to combine writing and paid work "during decades when there was no unemployment insurance, if we (and those close to us) were out of work, no food stamps, no medicare, no social security or welfare for parents or others who might become dependent."[19] Despite the "crushing" burden of her economic situation, significantly compounded by her oppression as woman and as lesbian, Gidlow continued to write—and to fill in one chunk of an historical tradition of lesbian poetry.

No less valuable in beginning to put together that mosaic is Angelina Weld Grimké, whose unpublished work provides solid documentation of the forces that buried her own life and poetry—and certainly those of other lesbians of color who might have written poetry. As Hull writes:

> The question—to repeat it—is: What did it mean to be a Black Lesbian/poet in America at the beginning of the twentieth century? First, it meant that you wrote (or half wrote)—in isolation—a lot which you did not show and knew you could not publish. It meant that when you did write to be printed, you did so in shackles—chained between the real experience you wanted to say and the conventions that would not give you voice. It meant that you fashioned a few race and nature poems, transliterated lyrics, and double-tongued verses which—sometimes (racism being what it is)—got published. It meant, finally, that you stopped writing altogether, dying, no doubt, with your real gifts stifled within—and leaving behind (in a precious few cases) the little that manages to survive of your true self in fugitive pieces.[20]

While Grimké wrote in forms that were generally compatible with the white male literary definition of poetry, some other Black women (lacking

Grimké's economic advantages and formal education) did not. Blues lyrics have proved a rich source of lesbian expression. Bessie Jackson, for instance, did a song called "B.D. Blues" (Bull Dagger Blues) during her career (1923-1935), while Bessie Smith sang several songs with explicitly lesbian lyrics.[21] Along with the songs of working-class white women, song lyrics by Black women and other women of color need to be explored seriously *as poetry* in order to find expressions of lesbian experiences, sometimes by women who might not meet a 1980's definition of "lesbian," most often by women whose own lives we can learn little or nothing about.[22] Where necessary, women's song lyrics—and other poems or poetic fragments—will have to be translated so that the words of lesbians whose sole or primary language was Spanish or Navajo or any of the multitude of immigrant tongues will not remain lost to us.[23]

While we have survived as lesbians for centuries "without access to any knowledge of a tradition, a continuity, a social underpinning,"[24] that mode of survival is finally ending. The work has already begun that gives historical shape to our lives and our literature. Hopefully it will continue in directions that encompass the diversity of past and present lesbian poetry and lesbian existence.

IV.

In 1975, at a point at which this work had begun with full force, Joan Larkin and I self-published *Amazon Poetry: An Anthology of Lesbian Poetry*, under the imprint of Out & Out Books. A slender volume (112 pages and 38 poets) compared to *Lesbian Poetry: An Anthology, Amazon Poetry* appeared at a time that now seems long ago in terms of lesbian publishing: Violet Press was putting out its first two perfect-bound (as opposed to stapled) books of lesbian poetry; the Women's Press Collective and Diana Press were publishing frequently, prior to their merger and eventual folding; *Amazon Quarterly*, then the one widely distributed lesbian literary magazine, had just put out its final issue; and none of today's lesbian-feminist literary magazines—*Azalea, Conditions, Feminary, Sinister Wisdom*—had begun to appear.[25]

The poetry that has been written since the appearance of our 1975 anthology seemed to us to necessitate a new volume of lesbian poetry. Since no lesbian publisher existed until fairly recently with the printing and distribution capacity to reach our potential audience, Joan and I tried for a year and a half to sell the expanded anthology to a large commercial publisher. The proposed book was turned down by eleven publishing houses with a variety of comments: "limited scope" (Doubleday); "difficult to market" (Dutton); "quality . . . varies too greatly to justify the collection on the basis of poetics rather than of politics" (Harper & Row). A few of the publishers had already printed "a lesbian book" and were waiting to see how it sold. We were fortunate that during this time Persephone Press emerged as a viable publisher. Keeping the book within the lesbian community, rather than publishing with one of the white male publishing conglomerates, was attractive to us, especially given our own involvement in lesbian publishing—Joan as publisher of Out & Out Books, mine as one of the founding editors of *Conditions*.

While we have reprinted *Amazon Poetry*'s Dedication and Prefatory Note, both slightly revised, and used work by all of those lesbian contributors who chose inclusion, *Lesbian Poetry* has turned out to be a new book, not simply an expanded version of an old one. As in the early seventies, women poets have continued to come out; some of the poets published here—Paula Gunn Allen, Marilyn Hacker, Honor Moore, and others—had not identified themselves as lesbians when *Amazon Poetry* first appeared. Joan's and my work in lesbian publishing introduced us to many lesbian poets, those published in a range of lesbian and non-lesbian feminist publications, as well as many whose work we had seen only in manuscript. Our physical proximity to the Lesbian Herstory Archives enabled us to read through both unpublished manuscripts and less widely distributed periodicals and books. Reading through this poetry, we have been well aware that we were putting together a book that reflects our own poetic tastes and personal/political priorities, rather than one which could be seen in any way as "definitive." In the time lapse between editing and publication, we expect many poems to be published which, had we seen them earlier, we would have published. From this viewpoint, the very vitality of lesbian poetry alone makes any published effort less than totally up-to-date and comprehensive. It will, we hope, lead to the appearance of other anthologies compiled by other editors.

Even in the apparent inclusiveness of an anthology entitled *Lesbian Poetry*, there is considerable invisibility. Our list of lesbian poets is shorter, and therefore less broadly representative, than the list of poets known in our community as lesbians. We have included only poets who have indicated a willingness to be so identified. Considering the external realities—the threat of loss of one's children, one's job, one's political and/or literary credibility in non-lesbian circles—the decision against inclusion here is far less surprising than the decision made by a sizable number of poets who, here and elsewhere, are willing to acknowledge publicly their lesbianism.

From this perspective alone, *Lesbian Poetry* must be seen as a the tip of an iceberg. The presence in it, for example, of Jean Mollison, a 63-year-old woman from rural New York who has many poems that have previously been seen only by close friends, serves as a crucial reminder of the existence of those lesbians whose work we have not seen, but who might very well have been writing poetry for four decades or more. They too, no less than

Sappho and Angelina Weld Grimké and Elsa Gidlow, are a part of the tradition of lesbian poetry.

In reading the lesbian poetry in this anthology, we cannot afford to forget the background of silence and denial and oppression out of which a vital, visible lesbian poetry has stubbornly emerged. While this background is important because it is at the same time not very far behind us and still present, the appearance of *Lesbian Poetry*—like the appearance of other publications by women who clearly identify themselves as lesbians—affirms our diversity, our creativity, our strength, our determination to continue to struggle and survive in a hostile world.

Notes

[1] See Louise Bernikow's "Introduction" to *The World Split Open: Four Centuries of Women Poets in England and America, 1552-1950* (New York: Vintage, 1974), especially her comments regarding Katherine Philips, "The English Sappho" (1631-1664); Aphra Behn (1640-1689); and Christina Rosetti (1830-1894). See also the entry on Margaret Fuller in Jonathan Katz, *Gay American History: Lesbians and Gay Men in the U.S.A.* (New York: Crowell, 1976), pp.461-467; Josephine Donovan's "The Unpublished Love Poems of Sarah Orne Jewett," *Frontiers* (Fall, 1979), pp.26-31; Willa Cather's *April Twilights (1903)* (Lincoln: University of Nebraska Press, 1976); and Lillian Faderman's *Surpassing the Love of Men: Romantic Friendship and Love Between Women from the Renaissance to the Present* (New York: William Morrow, 1981).

[2] Dudley Fitts in his "Foreword" to *Sappho: A New Translation* by Mary Barnard (Berkeley: University of California Press, 1958), pp.vii-viii. Fitts goes on to say: "We have heard a great deal about Sappho, and we know almost nothing." [Has anyone who has read John Donne's heterosexual love poetry ever even suggested that only by going outside his poems to learn about the details of his life could we establish that he had been intimately involved with women?] For a discussion of Sappho's reputation since her death in 558 B.C.; the burning of her poems in the Eastern Roman Empire (c.380 A.D.) and Western Europe (eleventh century A.D.); and several distorting translations of her poems, see Dolores Klaich's "Sappho and the Lesbian Ghetto" in *Woman + Woman: Attitudes Toward Lesbianism* (New York: Morrow, 1974), pp.129-160.

[3] In "The Female World of Love and Ritual: Relations between Women in Nineteenth-Century America," Carroll Smith-Rosenberg writes: "The essential question is not whether these women had genital contact and can therefore be defined as heterosexual or homosexual. The twentieth-century tendency to view human love and sexuality within a dichotomized universe of deviance and normality, genitality and platonic love, is alien to the emotions and attitudes of the nineteenth century and fundamentally distorts the nature of these women's emotional interactions" (*Signs*, Vol.1, No.1, Autumn, 1975, p.8). I include Dickinson here because she wrote poetry that expresses profound emotional attachments to other women. For her and for other women who lived before this century, this seems to me to be the key issue, *not* whether her love for women was expressed sexually and regardless of the state of her relationships with men; I agree with Smith-Rosenberg that our definitions of lesbian and heterosexual, especially in the 1980's, have no applicability to an earlier period.

See, for example, poems 51, 84, 158, 346, 458, 494, 631, 727, 1219, 1249, 1414, 1568 in *The Complete Poems of Emily Dickinson*, ed. Thomas H. Johnson (Cambridge: Harvard University Press, 1955) and letters 73, 74, 88, 94, 172, 177, 222 in *The Letters of Emily Dickinson*, eds. Thomas H. Johnson and Theodora Ward (Cambridge: Harvard University Press, 1958). These letters are cited by Lillian Faderman in "Emily Dickinson's Letters to Sue Gilbert," *Massachusetts Review* (Summer, 1977), pp.197-225 and "Emily Dickinson's Homoerotic Poetry," *Higginson Journal*, 1978, No. 18, pp. 19-27. See also Frederick L. Morey, "Emily Dickinson's Elusive Lover," *Higginson Journal*, 1978, No. 18, pp. 28-34; Paula Bennett, "The Language of Love: Emily Dickinson's Homoerotic Poetry," *Gai Saber* (Spring, 1977), Vol. 1, No.1; Jennifer Woodul, "Much Madness is Divinest Sense," *The Furies* (February, 1972).

[4] *Rising Tides: 20th Century American Women Poets*, eds. Laura Chester and Sharon Barba (New York: Washington Square Press, 1973). *No More Masks! An Anthology of Poems by Women*, eds. Florence Howe and Ellen Bass (Garden City, New York: Doubleday Anchor, 1973).

[5] *Rising Tides*, p.280.

[6] *We Become New*, eds. Lucille Iverson and Kathryn Ruby (New York: Bantam, 1975).

[7] *The World Split Open*, pp.14-15.

[8] May Sarton, *A World of Light: Portraits and Celebrations* (New York: Norton, 1976), p.22.

[9] Swenson, "To Confirm a Thing," *Amazon Poetry: An Anthology of Lesbian Poetry*, eds. Elly Bulkin and Joan Larkin (Brooklyn, New York: Out & Out Books, 1975), p.81. "To Confirm a Thing" was originally published in Swenson's *Another Animal: Poems* (New York: Scribner's, 1954). See also "Poet to Tiger" and "Deciding" in *New & Selected Things Taking Place* (New York: Atlantic-Little, Brown, 1978).

[10] *The Ladder* was published by the Daughters of Bilitis from 1956 to 1970; it was published independently until 1972 when it ceased publication. A reprint of the complete *Ladder* was issued in 1975 by Arno Press (New York). *Lesbiana, Book Reviews from the Ladder* (1976), edited by Barbara Grier, is available for $5.00 from Naiad Press, P.O. Box 10543, Tallahassee, FL 32302; *Lesbian Lives, Biographies of Women from the Ladder; The Lavender Herring, Lesbian Essays from the Ladder;* and *Lesbians Home Journal, Stories from the Ladder*, all edited by Barbara Grier and Coletta Reid, were published by Diana Press (1976). Editor of *The Ladder* from 1968 to 1972 and a frequent contributor for most of the life of the magazine, Barbara Grier wrote most frequently under the name of Gene Damon, as well as under a number of other pseudonyms.

[11] In *Gay American History*, Jonathan Katz documents "the simultaneous witch-hunting of 'perverts' and 'subversives' . . . taking place" from 1950-1955 (p.91). A supporter of Senator Joseph McCarthy, Senator Kenneth Wherry, Republican floor leader, is quoted in a July 17, 1950 *New York Post* interview with Max Lerner: "'You can't hardly separate homosexuals from subversives,' the Senator told me. 'Mind you, I don't say every subversive is a homosexual. But a man of low morality is a menace in the government, whatever he is, and they are all tied up together'" (p. 95). In the same interview, he says: "You can stretch the security risk further if you want to. . . but right now I want to start with the homosexuals. When we get through with them, then we'll see what comes next" (p. 96).

[12] All quotes are from the Vintage edition. See also Judith McDaniel's "A Conversation with Muriel Rukeyser," *New Women's Times Feminist Review* (April 25-May 8, 1980), pp. 4-5, 18-19.

[13] *To Lesbians Everywhere* (New York: Violet Press, 1976), pp.42-43.

[14] Unpublished material and discussions with Judith McDaniel. Rich, *Signs,* Vol.5, No.4 (Summer, 1980), 648. Rich writes: "I mean the term *lesbian continuum* to include a range—through each woman's life and throughout history—of woman-identified experience; not simply the fact that a woman has had or consciously desired genital sexual experience with another woman. If we expand it to embrace many more forms of primary intensity between and among women, including the sharing of a rich inner life, the bonding against male tyranny, the giving and receiving of practical and political support; if we can also hear it in such associations as *marriage resistance* and the 'haggard' behavior identified by Mary Daly . . . we begin to grasp breadths of female history and psychology which have lain out of reach as a consequence of limited, mostly clinical, definitions of 'lesbianism' " (648-649).

[15] Hull, " 'Under the Days': The Buried Life of Angelina Weld Grimké," *Conditions: Five, The Black Women's Issue* (1979), pp.17-25.

[16] Conversation with Paula Gunn Allen; see also her article, "Beloved Women: The Lesbian in American Indian Culture," *Conditions: Seven* (1981). Jacqueline Higgins Rosebrook makes the same point regarding loss of power in "Look What You've Done to My Song," *Heresies No. 10* (1980), p.84.

[17] Noda, letter to the author, October 4, 1978. See also Barbara Noda, Kitty Tsui, and Zee Wong, "Coming Out: We Are Here in the Asian Community: A Dialogue with Three Asian Women," *Bridge*, Vol.7, No.1 (Spring, 1979), pp.22-24.

[18] Gidlow, "Footprints in the Sands of the Sacred," *Frontiers*, Vol.IV, No.3 (1979), pp.48-49.

[19] Gidlow, p.50.

[20] Hull, p.20. See also Audre Lorde, "Scratching the Surface: Some Notes on Barriers to Women and Loving," *Black Scholar*, Vol.9, No.7 (April, 1978), pp.31-35. Barbara Smith writes: "Black women are still in the position of having to 'imagine,' discover and verify Black lesbian literature because so little has been written from an avowedly lesbian perspective. The near non-existence of Black lesbian literature which other Black lesbians and I so deeply feel has everything to do with the politics of our lives, the total suppression of identity that all Black women, lesbian and not, must face" ("Toward a Black Feminist Criticism," *Conditions: Two* [Fall, 1977], p.39).

[21] Bernikow includes blues lyrics and protest songs of working women in *The World Split Open*, although none of the songs she cites has lesbianism as a theme. "B.D. Blues" is available on *When Women Sang the Blues* and on *AC/DC Blues: Gay Jazz Reissues*. In Chris Albertson's discussion of Bessie Smith in *Gay American History*, he quotes "The Boy in the Boat": "When you see two women walking hand in hand,/Just look 'em over and try to understand . . ." (p.76).

[22] Paul Lauter's "Working-Class Women's Literature—An Introduction to Study" contains a lengthy bibliography (*Radical Teacher* [December, 1979], pp. 16-26).

[23] Rich, p.649.

[24] *Azalea*, A Magazine By & For Third World Lesbians is available from 306 Lafayette Ave., Brooklyn, NY 11238 ($6/4 issues; $10 institutional subscriptions; $2/single issue; free to women in prison—make checks payable to J.Gibbs). Information about these other lesbian magazines is included under Works by Contributors. The most up-to-date information about lesbian periodicals is in the Media Report to Women *Index/Directory of Women's Media* ($8 from Women's Institute for Freedom of the Press, 3306 Ross Place, NW, Washington, DC 20008).

Lesbian POETRY

an anthology

Elsa Gidlow

For the Goddess Too Well Known

I have robbed the garrulous streets,
Thieved a fair girl from their blight,
I have stolen her for a sacrifice
That I shall make to this night.

I have brought her, laughing,
To my quietly dreaming garden.
For what will be done there
I ask no man pardon.

I brush the rouge from her cheeks,
Clean the black kohl from the rims
Of her eyes; loose her hair;
Uncover the glimmering, shy limbs.

I break wild roses, scatter them over her.
The thorns between us sting like love's pain.
Her flesh, bitter and salt to my tongue,
I taste with endless kisses and taste again.

At dawn I leave her
Asleep in my wakening garden.
(For what was done there
I ask no man pardon.)

1919

Cunts Have Faces: Dialogue Among Rumpled Sheets

Cunts have faces
Did you know?

Faces without eyes?

Not if you know how to *see.*
It's the faces flowers have:
Violets, pansies
Neat virginal ones like daisies
Inviting the most fastidious bees.
Pale fleshy ones on big blondes—
Those strong-odored jasmine or gardenia types
Or some of the desert flowers
Drawing the night moths.
Reticent ones fertilized by indirection
Sensuous dramatic ones
Like jack-in-the-pulpit
And real man-eaters
Venus flytraps: dick traps.

Rolling in laughter
And rumpled sheets,
Pulling one over her—
Modest:
How do I know what you'll see here?

That's easy: a tiger lily
Reserve   then fire
Cool passion   contradictions
Fascinating contradictions
Artemis   hunting—yet fleeing
Won, you return—don't you?—
To virginity
After fulfilment   self-containment
In proportion to surrender,
Not remaining a gaping orifice
Reproaching the lover with
Never giving enough.
Finishing, you close up
Like escholchia at sundown.

1979

May Sarton

The Muse as Medusa

I saw you once, Medusa; we were alone.
I looked you straight in the cold eye, cold.
I was not punished, was not turned to stone—
How to believe the legends I am told?

I came as naked as any little fish,
Prepared to be hooked, gutted, caught;
But I saw you, Medusa, made my wish,
And when I left you I was clothed in thought . . .

Being allowed, perhaps, to swim my way
Through the great deep and on the rising tide,
Flashing wild streams, as free and rich as they,
Though you had power marshaled on your side.

The fish escaped to many a magic reef;
The fish explored many a dangerous sea—
The fish, Medusa, did not come to grief,
But swims still in a fluid mystery.

Forget the image: your silence is my ocean,
And even now it teems with life. You chose
To abdicate by total lack of motion,
But did it work, for nothing really froze?

It is all fluid still, that world of feeling
Where thoughts, those fishes, silent, feed and rove;
And, fluid, it is also full of healing,
For love is healing, even rootless love.

I turn your face around! It is my face.
That frozen rage is what I must explore—
Oh secret, self-enclosed, and ravaged place!
This is the gift I thank Medusa for.

1962

Jean Mollison

Do you remember now the night that we,
Empassioned by denial and at odds
With a strange love that would not set us free,
Rejected all our angry little gods?
The Devil's fury could not loose such storms
As those that since have surged inside of me;
Nor stocked my mind with more provoking forms,
Each one assigned to some cute treachery,
As day and night and night and day I still
Can hear your voice, can see your eyes, can feel,
When soft earth warms beneath us on the hill,
Old ties go under as the senses reel.
Oh, that is where I still am most undone!
For peace with angry gods is sorely won.

1942

It seems unlikely that we'll talk again
Walking side by side in morning cold,
And disagree on merits of the rain,
And how we want to die before we're old.
It seems unlikely that we can renew
The rapture that Millay wrote down for us;
Or that I will recite again to you
'Only the diamond and the diamond's dust . . .'
But when at every turn I find some trace
Of what was ours, now dispossessed and bare;
And where you stood, a smiling stranger's face
And where you whispered, only silence there,
It seems unlikely time will ever see
Destruction of our mock eternity.

1942

'Only the diamond and the diamond's dust'—sonnet CLVII by Edna St. Vincent Millay, originally published in *Wine From These Grapes* (1934).

Adrienne Rich

To Judith, Taking Leave

for J.H.

Dull-headed, with dull fingers
I patch once more
the pale brown envelope
still showing under ink scratches
the letterhead of MIND.
A chorus of old postmarks
echoes across its face.
It looks so frail
to send so far
and I should tear it across
mindlessly
and find another.
But I'm tired, can't endure
a single new motion
or room or object,
so I cling to this too
as if your tallness moving
against the rainlight
in an Amsterdam flat
might be held awhile
by a handwritten label
or a battered envelope
from your desk.

Once somewhere else
I shan't talk of you
as a singular event
or a beautiful thing I saw
though both are true.
I shan't falsify you
through praising and describing
as I shall other
things I have loved
almost as much.
There in Amsterdam
you'll be living as I
have seen you live

and as I've never seen you.
And I can trust
no plane to bring you
my life out there
in turbid America—
my own life, lived against
facts I keep there.

It wasn't literacy—
the right to read MIND—
or suffrage—to vote
for the lesser of two
evils—that were
the great gains, I see now,
when I think of all those women
who suffered ridicule
for us.
But this little piece of ground,
Judith! that two women
in love to the nerves' limit
with two men—
shared out in pieces
to men, children, memories
so different and so draining—
should think it possible
now for the first time
perhaps, to love each other
neither as fellow-victims
nor as a temporary
shadow of something better.
Still shared-out as we are,
lovers, poets, warmers
of men and children
against our flesh, not knowing
from day to day
what we'll fling out on the water
or what pick up
there at the tide's lip,
often tired, as I'm tired now
from sheer distances of soul
we have in one day to cover—
still to get here
to this little spur or headland
and feel now free enough

to leave our weapons somewhere
else–such are the secret
outcomes of revolution!
that two women can meet
no longer as cramped sharers
of a bitter mutual secret
but as two eyes in one brow
receiving at one moment
the rainbow of the world.

1962

Phantasia for Elvira Shatayev

(leader of a women's climbing team, all of whom died in a storm on Lenin Peak, August 1974. Later, Shatayev's husband found and buried the bodies.)

The cold felt cold until our blood
grew colder   then the wind
died down and we slept

If in this sleep I speak
it's with a voice no longer personal
(I want to say   *with voices*)
When the wind tore   our breath from us at last
we had no need of words
For months   for years   each one of us
had felt her own *yes*   growing in her
slowly forming   as she stood at windows   waited
for trains   mended her rucksack   combed her hair
What we were to learn   was simply   what we had
up here   as out of all words   that *yes*   gathered
its forces   fused itself   and only just in time
to meet a *No* of no degrees
the black hole   sucking the world in

I feel you climbing toward me
your cleated bootsoles leaving   their geometric bite
colossally embossed   on microscopic crystals
as when I trailed you in the Caucasus

Now I am further
ahead than either of us dreamed anyone would be
I have become

the white snow packed like asphalt by the wind
the women I love lightly flung against the mountain
that blue sky
our frozen eyes unribboned through the storm
we could have stitched that blueness together like a quilt

You come (I know this) with your love your loss
strapped to your body with your tape-recorder camera
ice-pick against advisement
to give us burial in the snow and in your mind
While my body lies out here
flashing like a prism into your eyes
how could you sleep You climbed here for yourself
we climbed for ourselves

When you have buried us told your story
ours does not end we stream
into the unfinished the unbegun
the possible
Every cell's core of heat pulsed out of us
into the thin air of the universe
the armature of rock beneath these snows
this mountain which has taken the imprint of our minds
through changes elemental and minute
as those we underwent
to bring each other here
choosing ourselves each other and this life
whose every breath and grasp and further foothold
is somewhere still enacted and continuing

In the diary I wrote: *Now we are ready*
and each of us knows it I have never loved
like this I have never seen
my own forces so taken up and shared
and given back
After the long training the early sieges
we are moving almost effortlessly in our love

In the diary as the wind began to tear
at the tents over us I wrote:
We know now we have always been in danger
down in our separateness
and now up here together but till now
we had not touched our strength

In the diary torn from my fingers I had written:
What does love mean
what does it mean "to survive"
A cable of blue fire ropes our bodies
burning together in the snow We will not live
to settle for less We have dreamed of this
all of our lives

1974

A Woman Dead in Her Forties

1.
Your breasts/ sliced-off The scars
dimmed as they would have to be
years later

All the women I grew up with are sitting
half-naked on rocks in sun
we look at each other and
are not ashamed

and you too have taken off your blouse
but this was not what you wanted:

to show your scarred, deleted torso

I barely glance at you
as if my look could scald you
though I'm the one who loved you

I want to touch my fingers
to where your breasts had been
but we never did such things

You hadn't thought everyone
would look so perfect
unmutilated

you pull on
your blouse again: stern statement:

There are things I will not share
with everyone

2.
You send me back to share
my own scars   first of all
with myself

What did I hide from her
what have I denied her
what losses suffered

how in this ignorant body
did she hide

waiting for her release
till uncontrollable light began to pour

from every wound and suture
and all the sacred openings

3.
Wartime.   We sit on warm
weathered, softening grey boards

the ladder glimmers where you told me
the leeches swim

I smell the flame
of kerosene   the pine

boards where we sleep side by side
in narrow cots

the night-meadow exhaling
its darkness   calling

child into woman
child into woman
woman

4.
Most of our love from the age of nine
took the form of jokes and mute

loyalty: you fought a girl
who said she'd knock me down

we did each other's homework
wrote letters   kept in touch, untouching

lied about our lives: I wearing
the face of the proper marriage

you the face of the independent woman
We cleaved to each other across that space

fingering webs
of love and estrangement   till the day

the gynecologist touched your breast
and found a palpable hardness

5.
You played heroic, necessary
games with death

since in your neo-protestant tribe the void
was supposed not to exist

except as a fashionable concept
you had no traffic with

I wish you were here tonight   I want
to yell at you

Don't accept
Don't give in

But would I be meaning your brave
irreproachable life, you dean of women, or

your unfair, unfashionable, unforgivable
woman's death?

6.
You are every woman I ever loved
and disavowed

a bloody incandescent chord strung out
across years, tracts of space

How can I reconcile this passion
with our modesty

your calvinist heritage
my girlhood frozen into forms

how can I go on this mission
without you

you, who might have told me
everything you feel is true?

7.
Time after time in dreams you rise
reproachful

once from a wheelchair pushed by your father
across a lethal expressway

Of all my dead it's you
who come to me unfinished

You left me amber beads
strung with turquoise from an Egyptian grave

I wear them wondering
How am I true to you?

I'm half-afraid to write poetry
for you   who never read it much

and I'm left laboring
with the secrets and the silence

In plain language: I never told you how I loved you
we never talked at your deathbed of your death

8.
One autumn evening in a train
catching the diamond-flash of sunset

in puddles along the Hudson
I thought: *I understand*

life and death now, the choices
I didn't know your choice

or how by then you had no choice
how the body tells the truth in its rush of cells

Most of our love took the form
of mute loyalty

we never spoke at your deathbed of your death

but from here on
I want more crazy mourning, more howl, more keening

We stayed mute and disloyal
because we were afraid

I would have touched my fingers
to where your breasts had been
but we never did such things

1974-1977

Transcendental Etude

for Michelle Cliff

This August evening I've been driving
over backroads fringed with queen anne's lace
my car startling young deer in meadows—one
gave a hoarse intake of her breath and all
four fawns sprang after her
into the dark maples.
Three months from today they'll be fair game
for the hit-and-run hunters, glorying
in a weekend's destructive power,
triggers fingered by drunken gunmen, sometimes
so inept as to leave the shattered animal
stunned in her blood. But this evening deep in summer
the deer are still alive and free,
nibbling apples from early-laden boughs
so weighted, so englobed
with already yellowing fruit
they seem eternal, Hesperidean
in the clear-tuned, cricket-throbbing air.

Later I stood in the dooryard,
my nerves singing the immense
fragility of all this sweetness,
this green world already sentimentalized, photographed,
advertised to death. Yet, it persists
stubbornly beyond the fake Vermont
of antique barnboards glazed into discothèques,
artificial snow, the sick Vermont of children
conceived in apathy, grown to winters
of rotgut violence,
poverty gnashing its teeth like a blind cat at their lives.
Still, it persists. Turning off onto a dirt road
from the raw cuts bulldozed through a quiet village
for the tourist run to Canada,
I've sat on a stone fence above a great, soft, sloping field
of musing heifers, a farmstead
slanting its planes calmly in the calm light,
a dead elm raising bleached arms

above a green so dense with life,
minute, momentary life–slugs, moles, pheasants, gnats,
spiders, moths, hummingbirds, groundhogs, butterflies–
a lifetime is too narrow
to understand it all, beginning with the huge
rockshelves that underlie all that life.

No one ever told us we had to study our lives,
make of our lives a study, as if learning natural history
or music, that we should begin
with the simple exercises first
and slowly go on trying
the hard ones, practicing till strength
and accuracy became one with the daring
to leap into transcendence, take the chance
of breaking down in the wild arpeggio
or faulting the full sentence of the fugue.
–And in fact we can't live like that: we take on
everything at once before we've even begun
to read or mark time, we're forced to begin
in the midst of the hardest movement,
the one already sounding as we are born.
At most we're allowed a few months
of simply listening to the simple line
of a woman's voice singing a child
against her heart. Everything else is too soon,
too sudden, the wrenching-apart, that woman's heartbeat
heard ever after from a distance,
the loss of that ground-note echoing
whenever we are happy, or in despair.

Everything else seems beyond us,
we aren't ready for it, nothing that was said
is true for us, caught naked in the argument,
the counterpoint, trying to sightread
what our fingers can't keep up with, learn by heart
what we can't even read. And yet
it *is* this we were born to. We aren't virtuosi
or child prodigies, there are no prodigies
in this realm, only a half-blind, stubborn
cleaving to the timbre, the tones of what we are
–even when all the texts describe it differently.

And we're not performers, like Liszt, competing
against the world for speed and brilliance
(the 79-year-old pianist said, when I asked her
What makes a virtuoso?—Competitiveness.)
The longer I live the more I mistrust
theatricality, the false glamour cast
by performance, the more I know its poverty beside
the truths we are salvaging from
the splitting-open of our lives.
The woman who sits watching, listening,
eyes moving in the darkness
is rehearsing in her body, hearing-out in her blood
a score touched off in her perhaps
by some words, a few chords, from the stage:
a tale only she can tell.

But there come times—perhaps this is one of them—
when we have to take ourselves more seriously or die;
when we have to pull back from the incantations,
rhythms we've moved to thoughtlessly,
and disenthrall ourselves, bestow
ourselves to silence, or a deeper listening, cleansed
of oratory, formulas, choruses, laments, static
crowding the wires. We cut the wires,
find ourselves in free-fall, as if
our true home were the undimensional
solitudes, the rift
in the Great Nebula.
No one who survives to speak
new language, has avoided this:
the cutting-away of an old force that held her
rooted to an old ground
the pitch of utter loneliness
where she herself and all creation
seem equally dispersed, weightless, her being a cry
to which no echo comes or can ever come.

But in fact we were always like this,
rootless, dismembered: knowing it makes the difference.
Birth stripped our birthright from us,
tore us from a woman, from women, from ourselves
so early on
and the whole chorus throbbing at our ears

like midges, told us nothing, nothing
of origins, nothing we needed
to know, nothing that could re-member us.

Only: that it is unnatural,
the homesickness for a woman, for ourselves,
for that acute joy at the shadow her head and arms
cast on a wall, her heavy or slender
thighs on which we lay, flesh against flesh,
eyes steady on the face of love; smell of her milk, her sweat,
terror of her disappearance, all fused in this hunger
for the element they have called most dangerous, to be
lifted breathtaken on her breast, to rock within her
—even if beaten back, stranded again, to apprehend
in a sudden brine-clear thought
trembling like the tiny, orbed, endangered
egg-sac of a new world:
This is what she was to me, and this
is how I can love myself—
as only a woman can love me.

Homesick for myself, for her—as, after the heatwave
breaks, the clear tones of the world
manifest: cloud, bough, wall, insect, the very soul of light:
homesick as the fluted vault of desire
articulates itself: *I am the lover and the loved,*
home and wanderer, she who splits
firewood and she who knocks, a stranger
in the storm, two women, eye to eye
measuring each other's spirit, each other's
limitless desire,
a whole new poetry beginning here.

Vision begins to happen in such a life
as if a woman quietly walked away
from the argument and jargon in a room
and sitting down in the kitchen, began turning in her lap
bits of yarn, calico and velvet scraps,
laying them out absently on the scrubbed boards
in the lamplight, with small rainbow-colored shells
sent in cotton-wool from somewhere far away,
and skeins of milkweed from the nearest meadow—
original domestic silk, the finest findings—

and the darkblue petal of the petunia,
and the dry darkbrown lace of seaweed;
not forgotten either, the shed silver
whisker of the cat,
the spiral of paper-wasp-nest curling
beside the finch's yellow feather.
Such a composition has nothing to do with eternity,
the striving for greatness, brilliance—
only with the musing of a mind
one with her body, experienced fingers quietly pushing
dark against bright, silk against roughness,
pulling the tenets of a life together
with no mere will to mastery,
only care for the many-lived, unending
forms in which she finds herself,
becoming now the sherd of broken glass
slicing light in a corner, dangerous
to flesh, now the plentiful, soft leaf
that wrapped round the throbbing finger, soothes the wound;
and now the stone foundation, rockshelf further
forming underneath everything that grows.

1977

Transit

> *1. a) passage through or across. b) a transition; change . . . .*
> *4.* in astronomy, *a) the apparent passage of a heavenly body across a given meridian or through the field of a telescope.*
> *(Webster)*

When I meet the skier she is always
walking, skis and poles shouldered, toward the mountain
free-swinging in worn boots
over the path new-sifted with fresh snow
her greying dark hair almost hidden by
a cap of many colors
her fifty-year-old, strong, impatient body
dressed for cold and speed
her eyes level with mine

And when we pass each other I look into her face
wondering what we have in common
where our minds converge
for we do not pass each other, she passes me
as I halt beside the fence tangled in snow,
she passes me as I shall never pass her
in this life

Yet I remember us together
climbing Chocorua, summer nineteen forty-five
details of vegetation beyond the timberline
lichens, wildflowers, birds,
amazement where the trail broke out onto the granite ledge
sloped over blue lakes, green pines, giddy air
like dreams of flying

When sisters separate they haunt each other
as she, who I might once have been, haunts me
or is it I who do the haunting
halting and watching on the path
how she appears again through lightly-blowing
crystals, how her strong knees carry her,
how unaware she is, how simple
this is for her, how without let or hindrance
she travels in her body
until the point of passing, where the skier
and the cripple must decide
to recognize each other?

1979

Audre Lorde

Equinox

My daughter marks the day that spring begins.
I cannot celebrate spring without remembering
how the bodies of unborn children
bake in their mothers flesh like ovens
consecrated to the flame that eats them
lit by mobiloil and easternstandard
Unborn children in their blasted mothers
floating like small monuments
in an ocean of oil.

The year my daughter was born
DuBois died in Accra while I
marched into Washington
to a death knell of dreaming
which 250,000 others mistook for a hope
believing only Birmingham's black children
were being pounded into mortar in churches
that year
some of us still thought
Vietnam was a suburb of Korea.

Then John Kennedy fell off the roof
of Southeast Asia
and shortly afterward my whole house burned down
with nobody in it
and on the following sunday my borrowed radio announced
that Malcolm was shot dead
and I ran to reread
all that he had written
because death was becoming such an excellent measure
of prophecy
As I read his words the dark mangled children
came streaming out of the atlas
Hanoi Angola Guinea-Bissau Mozambique Pnam-Phen
merged into Bedford-Stuyvesant and Hazelhurst Mississippi
haunting my New York tenement that terribly bright summer
while Detroit and Watts and San Francisco were burning
I lay awake in stifling Broadway nights afraid
for whoever was growing in my belly

and suppose it started earlier than planned
who would I trust to take care that my daughter
did not eat poisoned roaches
when I was gone?

If she did, it doesn't matter
because I never knew it.
Today both children came home from school
talking about spring and peace
and I wonder if they will ever know it
I want to tell them we have no right to spring
because our sisters and brothers are burning
because every year the oil grows thicker
and even the earth is crying
because black is beautiful but currently
going out of style
that we must be very strong
and love each other
in order to go on living.

1967

Love Poem

Speak earth and bless me with what is richest
make sky flow honey out of my hips
rigid as mountains
spread over a valley
carved out by the mouth of rain.

And I knew when I entered her I was
high wind in her forests hollow
fingers whispering sound
honey flowed
from the split cup
impaled on a lance of tongues
on the tips of her breasts on her navel
and my breath
howling into her entrances
through lungs of pain.

Greedy as herring-gulls
or a child
I swing out over the earth
over and over
again.

1969

Black Mother Woman

I cannot recall you gentle
yet through your heavy love
I have become
an image of your once delicate flesh
split with deceitful longings.

When strangers come and compliment me
your aged spirit takes a bow
jingling with pride
but once you hid that secret
in the center of furies
hanging me
with deep breasts and wiry hair
with your own split flesh
and long suffering eyes
buried in myths of little worth.

But I have peeled away your anger
down to the core of love
and look mother
I Am
a dark temple where your true spirit rises
beautiful
and tough as chestnut
stanchion against your nightmare of weakness
and if my eyes conceal
a squadron of conflicting rebellions
I learned from you
to define myself
through your denials.

1972

To My Daughter the Junkie on a Train

Children we have not borne
bedevil us by becoming
themselves
painfully sharp and unavoidable
like a needle in our flesh.

Coming home on the subway from a PTA meeting
of minds committed like murder
or suicide
to their own private struggle
a long-legged girl with a horse in her brain
slumps down beside me
begging to be ridden asleep
for the price of a midnight train
free from desire.
Little girl on the nod
if we are measured by the dreams we avoid
then you are the nightmare
of all sleeping mothers
rocking back and forth
the dead weight of your arms
locked about our necks
heavier than our habit
of looking for reasons.

My corrupt concern will not replace
what you once needed
but I am locked into my own addictions
and offer you my help, one eye
out
for my own station.
Roused and deprived
your costly dream explodes
into a terrible technicoloured laughter
at my failure
up and down across the aisle
women avert their eyes
as the other mothers who became useless
curse their children who became junk.

1973

125th Street and Abomey

Head bent, walking through snow
I see you Seboulisa
printed inside the back of my head
like marks of the newly wrapped akai
that kept my sleep fruitful in Dahomey
and I poured onto the red earth in your honor
those ancient parts of me
most precious and least needed
my well-guarded past
the energy-eating secrets
I surrender to you as libation
mother, illuminate my offering
of old victories
over men over women over my selves
who has never before dared
to whistle into the night
take my fear of being alone
like my warrior sisters
who rode in defense of your queendom
disguised and apart
give me the woman strength
of tongue in this cold season.

Half earth and time splits us apart
like struck rock.
A piece lives elegant stories
too simply put
while a dream on the edge of summer
of brown rain in nim trees
snail shells from the dooryard
of King Toffah
brings me where my blood moves
Seboulisa mother goddess with one breast
eaten away by worms of sorrow and loss
see me now
your severed daughter
laughing our name into echo
all the world shall remember.

1974

Seboulisa—the goddess of Abomey, "The Mother of us all."
akai—narrow, wrapped braids.

—*A. L.*

Between Ourselves

Once when I walked into a room
my eyes would seek out the one or two black faces
for contact or reassurance or a sign
I was not alone
now walking into rooms full of black faces
that would destroy me for any difference
where shall my eyes look?
Once it was easy to know
who were my people.

If we were stripped to our strength
of all pretense
and our flesh was cut away
the sun would bleach all our bones as white
as the face of my black mother
was bleached white by gold
or Orishala
and how
does that measure me?

I do not believe
our wants have made all our lies
holy.

Under the sun on the shores of Elmina
a black man sold the woman who carried
my grandmother in her belly
he was paid with bright yellow coin
that shone in the evening sun
and in the faces of her sons and daughters.
When I see that brother behind my eyes
his irises are bloodless and without color
his tongue clicks like yellow coins
tossed up on this shore
where we share the same corner
of an alien and corrupted heaven
and whenever I try to eat
the words
of easy blackness as salvation
I taste the color
of my grandmother's first betrayal.

I do not believe
our wants
have made all our lies
holy.

But I do not whistle his name at the shrine of Shopona
I do not bring down the rosy juices of death upon him
nor forget Orishala
is called the god of whiteness
who works in the dark wombs of night
forming the shapes we all wear
so that even cripples and dwarfs and albinos
are sacred worshipers
when the boiled corn is offered.

Humility lies
in the face of history
I have forgiven myself
for him
for the white meat
we all consumed in secret
before we were born
we shared the same meal.
When you impale me
upon your lances of narrow blackness
before you hear my heart speak
mourn your own borrowed blood
your own borrowed visions.
Do not mistake my flesh for the enemy
do not write my name in the dust
before the shrine of the god of smallpox
for we are all children of Eshu
god of chance and the unpredictable
and we each wear many changes
inside of our skin.

Armed with scars
healed
in many different colors
I look into my own faces
as Eshu's daughter crying
if we do not stop killing
the other
in ourselves

the self we hate
in others
soon we shall all lie
in the same direction
and Eshidale's priests will be very busy
they who alone can bury
all those who seek their own death
by jumping up from the ground
and landing upon their heads.

1975

Orishala—a major *Orisha* (goddesses and gods of the Yoruba people of Western Nigeria and Dahomey).
Shopona—the *Orisha* of smallpox.
Eshu—son of Yemanja, goddess of oceans. Messenger between all of the *Orisha-Vodu* and humans. He knows their different languages and is an accomplished linguist who both transmits and interprets, a key function since the *Orisha* understand neither each other's language nor the language of humans. He is a male face of the goddess Afrekete.
Eshidale—a local *Orisha* of the Ife region of Nigeria.

—A. L.

Power

The difference between poetry and rhetoric
is being
ready to kill
yourself
instead of your children.

I am trapped on a desert of raw gunshot wounds
and a dead child dragging his shattered black
face off the edge of my sleep
blood from his punctured cheeks and shoulders
is the only liquid for miles and my stomach
churns at the imagined taste while
my mouth splits into dry lips
without loyalty or reason
thirsting for the wetness of his blood
as it sinks into the whiteness
of the desert where I am lost
without imagery or magic
trying to make power out of hatred and destruction
trying to heal my dying son with kisses
only the sun will bleach his bones quicker.

The policeman who shot down a 10-year-old in Queens
stood over the boy with his cop shoes in childish blood
and a voice said "Die you little motherfucker" and
there are tapes to prove that. At his trial
this policeman said in his own defense
"I didn't notice the size or nothing else
only the color." and
there are tapes to prove that, too.

Today that 37-year-old white man with 13 years of police forcing
has been set free
by 11 white men who said they were satisfied
justice had been done
and one black woman who said
"They convinced me" meaning
they had dragged her 4'10" black woman's frame
over the hot coals of four centuries of white male approval
until she let go the first real power she ever had
and lined her own womb with cement
to make a graveyard for our children.

I have not been able to touch the destruction within me.
But unless I learn to use
the difference between poetry and rhetoric
my power too will run corrupt as poisonous mold
or lie limp and useless as an unconnected wire
and one day I will take my teenaged plug
and connect it to the nearest socket
raping an 85-year-old white woman
who is somebody's mother
and as I beat her senseless and set a torch to her bed
a greek chorus will be singing in 3/4 time
"Poor thing. She never hurt a soul. What beasts they are."

1975

Need:
A Choral of Black Women's Voices

For Patricia Cowan and Bobbie Jean Graham and the 100's of other mangled Black Women whose nightmares inform my words

tattle tale tit
your tongue will be slit
and every little boy in town
shall have a little bit.
nursery rhyme

1.

I: This woman is Black
so her blood is shed into silence
this woman is Black
so her death falls to earth
like the drippings of birds
to be washed away with silence and rain.

P.C.: For a long time after the baby came
I didn't go out at all
and it got to be really lonely.
Then Bubba started asking about his father
I wanted to connect with the blood again
thought maybe I'd meet somebody
and we could move on together
help make the dream real.
An ad in the paper said
"Black actress needed
to audition in a play by Black playwright."
I was anxious to get back to work
thought this might be a good place to start
so on the way home from school with Bubba
I answered the ad.
He put a hammer through my head.

B.J.G.: If you are hit in the middle of your body
by a ten-ton truck
your caved-in chest bears the mark of a tire
and your liver pops
like a rubber ball.
If you are knocked down by boulders

from a poorly graded hill
your dying is stamped by the rockprint
upon your crushed body
by the impersonal weight of it all
while life drips out through your liver
smashed by the mindless stone.
When your boyfriend methodically beats you to death
in the alley behind your apartment
and the neighbors pull down their windowshades
because they don't want to get involved
the police call it a crime of passion
not a crime of hatred
but I still died
of a lacerated liver
and a man's heel
imprinted upon my chest.

I: Dead Black women haunt the black maled streets
paying the cities' secret and familiar tithe of blood
burn blood beat blood cut blood
seven year old child rape victim blood blood
of a sodomized grandmother blood blood
on the hands of my brother blood
and his blood clotting in the teeth of strangers
as women we were meant to bleed
but not this useless blood
my blood each month a memorial
to my unspoken sisters falling
like red drops to the asphalt
I am not satisfied to bleed
as a quiet symbol for no one's redemption
why is it our blood
that keeps these cities fertile?

I do not even know all their names.
My sisters deaths are not noteworthy
nor threatening enough to decorate the evening news
not important enough to be fossilized
between the right-to-life pickets
and the San Francisco riots for gay liberation
blood blood of my sisters fallen in this bloody war
with no names no medals no exchange of prisoners
no packages from home

no time off for good behaviour
no victories no victors

B.J.G.: Only us
kept afraid to walk out into moonlight
lest we touch our power
only us
kept afraid to speak out
lest our tongues be slit
for the witches we are
our chests crushed
by the foot of a brawny acquaintance
and a ruptured liver bleeding life onto the stones.

ALL: And how many other deaths
do we live through daily
pretending
we are alive?

2.

P.C.: What terror embossed my face onto your hatred
what ancient and unchallenged enemy
took on my flesh within your eyes
came armed against you
with laughter and a hopeful art
my hair catching the sunlight
my small son eager to see his mother at work?
Now my blood stiffens in the cracks
of your fingers raised to wipe
a half-smile from your lips.
In this picture of you
the face of a white policeman
bends
over my bleeding son
decaying into my brother
who stalked me with a singing hammer.

B.J.G.: And what do you need me for, brother,
to move for you, feel for you, die for you?
You have a grave need for me
but your eyes are thirsty for vengeance
dressed in the easiest blood
and I am closest.

P.C.: When you opened my head with your hammer
did the boogie stop in your brain
the beat go on
the terror run out of you like curdled fury
a half-smile upon your lips?
And did your manhood lay in my skull like a netted fish
or did it spill out like blood
like impotent fury off the tips of your fingers
as your sledgehammer clove my bone to let the light out
did you touch it as it flew away?

ALL: Borrowed hymns veil the misplaced hatred
saying you need me you need me you need me
like a broken drum
calling me black goddess black hope black strength
black mother
you touch me
and I die in the alleys of Boston
with a stomach stomped through the small of my back
a hammered-in skull in Detroit
a ceremonial knife through my grandmother's used vagina
my burned body hacked to convenience in a vacant lot
I lie in midnight blood like a rebel city
bombed into false submission
and our enemies still sit in power
and judgement
over us all.

P.C.: *I need you.*
Was there no place left
to plant your hammer
spend anger rest horror
no other place to dig for your manhood
except in my woman's brain?

B.J.G.: Do you need me submitting to terror at nightfall
to chop into bits and stuff warm into plastic bags
near the neck of the Harlem River
and they found me there
swollen with your need
do you need me to rape in my seventh year
till blood breaks the corners of my child's mouth
and you explain I was being seductive.

ALL: Do you need me to print on our children
the destruction our enemies imprint upon you
like a Mack truck or an avalanche
destroying us both
carrying home their hatred
you are re-learning my value
in an enemy coin.

3.

I: I am wary of need
that tastes like destruction.
I am wary of need that tastes like destruction.
Who ever learns to love me
from the mouth of my enemies
walks the edge of my world
like a phantom in a crimson cloak
and the dreambooks speak of money
but my eyes say death.

The simplest part of this poem
is the truth in each one of us
to which it is speaking.
How much of this truth can I bear to see
and still live
unblinded?
How much of this pain
can I use?

ALL: *"We cannot live without our lives."*
"We cannot live without our lives."

1979

Patricia Cowan—21, bludgeoned to death in Detroit, 1978.
Bobbie Jean Graham—34, beaten to death in Boston, 1979. One of 12 Black women murdered within a 3-month period in that city.
"We cannot live without our lives"—title of book by Barbara Deming.

—*A. L.*

Clare Coss

Emma

This summer I dreamed that Emma Goldman
came to a theatre workshop.
She was quite hepped up about
what was happening at fifth avenue and fiftieth street
for instance
across from the cathedral and down the street from Bergdorf's.
She wanted to make certain that we were politically aware
of the implications of our existence.
So she marched out into the center of our workspace
wearing a long dark cape
high boots and white petticoats that
frothed at the bottom of her heavy skirt
as she kicked the stage clear of crates and claptrap
and adjusted her glasses with a quick push of an index finger.

Before anyone could put her through the questioner
she snapped
"You there: climb the walls
You there: beat your breast
You there: prostrate yourself before atlas holding up
the world right smack in the middle of rockefeller center
at fifth avenue and fiftieth street.

And don't tell me that if I want to lecture the audience
I should write a political tract
because what you have here is character and situation.

You there: repeat the word collectivity fast
until it sounds like the hoofbeats of a horse running wild
with the news that we are all
up against the wall of economic oppression.
Because what you have here is character and situation
and the potential for women who are moving together
to move away from just carving out for themselves
a bigger piece of the capitalist pie."

What becomes a legend most?
Her visions.
Her life's work.

Her hard realities.

And I dreamed that the world's womanline rose up
to occupy rockefeller center
which came to be known as the new york based world wide
women's center for international peace and equal justice
and clean air and water
and the very fish in the sea
leaped up and splashed the ozone layer with their joy
because finally
mere anarchy was loosed upon the land.

Needless to say, atlas never got it up again.

1976

the questioner—a theater research form used to elicit thematic material.

She Is an Older Person Now

my mother
even in her encroaching senility
continues to be physically erotic
sitting on a plain wooden chair
before the bathroom sink
naked
she takes an hour at her bath
each evening
covering her body wih irish spring
scrubbing her legs with a tough little brush
(a new ritual
she claims it came from me
where did she get this notion)
then going over her body
with an almost dripping washcloth
to remove the irish spring
drying rubbing dry carefully
she sits naked at her bath
on a wooden chair
each evening it begins to take
a little longer
(I haven't watched

just handed her the talc
in through the door
and glimpsed her changed
now older person's body)

your bath   you at your bath
I recall
my sock-stockinged right foot
as I lie back on her bed
rubbing up and down her left hip
as she stands facing me and talks
compulsively in repetitious tones
with long hesitations
straining to hold on to the thought
a thought
we are like two great cats
I hadn't realized my own pleasure
and satisfaction as her hand
rested lightly on my foot
moving up and down with caressing rubs
on her left side

mommy
you were always
always always
so physically erotic with me
so much so that I
can be
with you
after a six-month absence
and within a few minutes
this spontaneous touching flows between us
felt but
not noticed
until now
how our bodies continue to speak easily
though our minds have trouble

your bath   you at your bath
reminded me to notice
how we can sometimes
for a few minutes
be
touching

1977

Frankie Hucklenbroich

Genealogy

There was of course
my father. My old man.
Out of some back-country Polish pride
wanting to be called 'Dad'. (A firm
and friendly word. A man-to-man.)
Poor soul, he longed for sons, and bred four women,
and never liked to hear the word 'Papa'.
He stood behind the big black barberchair,
supporting us all on 60¢ haircuts,
looking like a 1940's movie hero,
and holding in his left hand the comb for all the world;
in his right, the steel barber-shears,
cutting, cutting, cutting.

1974

Due Process

After having been acquitted by a hung jury
of the charge of murdering my mother
I wrote three novels, seven poems, and
an essay on the subject, thus vastly
improving my wardrobe and the chances
for the Equal Rights Amendment

A lot of invitations
to dinner-parties find me, and I still
get phone calls from the matron on Ward G
and I've just been asked to address the League
of Lizzie Borden Lovers' annual convention
in the fall. Honey,
don't worry about

dying in bed, about being found dead
in my bed, with your long legs
gripping my throat
We'll do just fine together

and you can help me bury my mother's hands
almost nightly

1974

For All the Lovers Among Us

For all the lovers among us, bloated with dreams
I've decided to issue a warning about those rare bitches
who stand like stars inside their particular darkness
I will, of course, include certain appropriate phrases
Say things like 'deep as wind' and 'raw-boned as ivy'
Also: 'The nubs on their shoulders keep promising wings to be grown'

Someone must stop these women. There are too many days
when they just don't go by the script, until nobody much
can count on directives, or even a manual
for wayward backtracking. It's bloody
unfair

For example, I know I'm going to want you
to stay and watch the late movie
even if it is just Roy and Dale. Along with the grass and cold beer
and a pillow to hold your wild hair, I'll throw in my talk
(but only during commercials). Sitting beside you always turns me
nervous as snakes' skin and naive as a tame rat.
Beyond this, love freezes. Though your eyes
are dark and slow and lazy, at the end, we will not
even touch hands

I never expected any overt romance, or very much concern
but Roy and Dale would be scandalized
and I used to know a cigar-store Indian
that was softer-hearted than you

1975

Lynn Strongin

Sayre
(Woman Professor)

The men in her department envied her.
She was too handsome, had published too many poems.
So, she'd tone down:

she wore olive-drab all that autumn
said she was in a dry season
could not write a single poem.

Hand-to-hip she'd
breathe in the air
of evening. The casual woman.

Sayre!
She'd claim she was a lonely woman
and besides had a bad spine. Who'd envy her?

So intense that her fist
would smash glass
a Sunday evening.

But she'd flush a whole nest of quail
out of hiding
without so much as a shotgun (or a sound)

Camouflaged
broods of poems came.
The poem for her was—love's occasion.

She'd rise after, with that radiance
of a woman to meet her lover, eye shining
face to face.

Not one of the men guessed it was another woman.
So handsomely she moved, so darkly as through glass.

1971

Joan Larkin

Song

for female voices

Suddenly nothing is coming right.
My lovely child has become fat.
Her face is red with ugly scabs.
Love, does it mean I am a bad

Mummy, please stay with me.
Don't go to work today.
My tummy hurts. I want
milk in my bottle. I want

mother? I wanted to be a great
authoress. Or author's mistress—
I am always late to work. Always
I wanted to be a perfect woman,

you to lie down with me.
I peed again in bed—
my daddy never yells.
Now you're making me cry.

a mother, big, with wonderful dinners
in the pot, and children I only sing to,
a woman woven of different threads:
flat in the kitchen, but in bed

I only want my daddy.
Can't he take care of me?
He calls me his little
baby and tucks me in.

I'll play a lute of long hair
and little nightgown; I'll move
like a soft-coated animal; the moon
will be drawn to touch my body in love.

I want my blanket. Please,
can't we go to the zoo?

When I'm big I'll get real babies.
Then I'll be just like you.

1974

Rhyme of My Inheritance

My mother gave me a bitter tongue.
My father gave me a turned back.
My grandmother showed me her burned hands.
My brother showed me a difficult book.
These were their gifts; the rest was talk.

I discovered my body in the dark.
It had a surprise in its little crack.
I started to say what I'd found in the dark,
but my mother gave me a dirty look
and my father turned a key in the lock.

I was left alone with the difficult book
and the stove that burned my grandmother's hands,
and while they muttered behind my back
I learned to read and to make my bread,
to eat my words and lie flat in my bed.

They took me to school where I learned to be cute:
I wore clean jumpers and washed my hands;
I put my hands up to cover my mouth;
I listened to everything everyone said
and kept what I could in my stuffed-up head.

I had weeping eyes and a chest that coughed,
a stomach that hurt, and a mouth that laughed
whether or not I felt good or bad.
I was always promoted to the next grade.
I graduated; I got laid.

I did what girls were supposed to do.
I wore a white dress; I was photographed;
my teeth were perfect, my knees were crossed.
I cleaned up the mess that the baby made.

I hope that my body's price is paid.

I'm giving the gifts back, one by one.
I'm tearing the pages of my past.
I'm turning my back. I'm turning them down.
I'm burning their strict house to the ground.
May I never want bread at their table again.

May I let go of these bitter rhymes;
and may this burial be my last
while I live in my body and learn from my bones
to make some less predictable sound.
Let this coffin of verses inherit my pain.

1975

"Vagina" Sonnet

Is "vagina" suitable for use
in a sonnet? I don't suppose so.
A famous poet told me, "Vagina's ugly."
Meaning, of course, the *sound* of it. In poems.
Meanwhile, he inserts his penis frequently
into his verse, calling it, seriously, "My
Penis." It *is* short, I know, and dignified.
I mean of course the sound of it. In poems.
This whole thing is unfortunate, but petty,
like my hangup concerning English Dept. memos
headed "Mr./Mrs./Miss"—only a fishbone
in the throat of the revolution—
a waste of brains—to be concerned about
this minor issue of my cunt's good name.

1975

Some Unsaid Things

I was not going to say
how you lay with me

nor where your hands went
& left their light impressions

nor whose face was white
as a splash of moonlight

nor who spilled the wine
nor whose blood stained the sheet

nor which one of us wept
to set the dark bed rocking

nor what you took me for
nor what I took you for

nor how your fingertips
in me were roots

light roots torn leaves put down—
nor what you tore from me

nor what confusion came
of our twin names

nor will I say whose body
opened, sucked, whispered

like the ocean, unbalancing
what had seemed a safe position

1975

Stop

I hate it when you
fill my glass up
without asking me.

I always liked
a little
on a plate
in a cup

an egg
with space around it
an orange
with a knife
next to it

a cup
with space above
the coffee

discrete colors
orange   pewter   black

the porcelain glaze on the china
the blue napkin.

I want to keep things
separate. I hate it
when you break my egg.
I hate when you salt things
when you assume
I want cream

or the shade down
or touch, or looks
of kindness.

I want nothing
to lose
its cutting edge
nothing
to run together.

You had better
stop
pouring yourself
into my glass.

1975

Notations—the F Train

for Deborah Dickson

Kool I
Bruce
Head 155
Steam One
Chino
Gonzo 22

What is scrawled on the subway walls
is a certain notion of strength.

there is also the strength of water
that flows (around the rock)
that flows (over the stone)
that carries with itself
leaf and leaf and leaf
the letters of green lives

The station at West 4th Street
smells of smoke; I notice it tonight.

It is 2 o'clock.

There are two women with dyed, worried faces
and hard hair, the color of dolls' wigs
standing together in coats that mimic fur.

They are the only other women
in this night station of men—
men lounging and watching, chewing gum,
reading their Sunday paper,
some with thumbs in their trousers,

with keys, with umbrellas
striding the platform.
One man stands by a post and vomits
and vomits and vomits.

No one seems to be taking
notice of anyone
except a few whose eyes
let me see that I am alone here.
At this hour, women do not travel.

water
travels
without stopping
falls, both hitting the stone
and flowing over the stone
making the unstopped
music of water
its continuous going
over the earth and through it
wearing the rock
the rock   the rock
softening
everything on earth that is hard
a certain notion of strength

I may not let my eyes meet
their eyes, on the train to Brooklyn.
That is a sort of invitation.

There is a joke the cops in my neighborhood
shared with certain women
during the most recent rape scare.
It was that the victims
had found the rapist desirable
and had asked for it anyway
by being out on the street at night.

Where were you going anyway?
they asked my sister,
who was—and this is a fact—
on her way to a meeting about the survival of earth,

but who, between 9 and 11,
was walked to the park at gunpoint,
raped,
then told to turn her back at the fence
where she clung, waiting
maybe to be murdered,
while the man who had just raped her
ran
into the darkness.

water
runs
it is a certain notion of strength
a woman has revealed in a film
which she made by allowing the time
to look at water
moving
to listen to the sound of water
hour after hour after hour
after hour after hour
keeping her eyes on the water
and holding it with her camera

They were asking my sister
the tour guide
Where can I find a woman?
My home, so far away.
I have need for a woman.
What are you doing tonight?
I have need, have need, have need.
Where can I find a woman?

On the subway wall, I see the sentence
I doin' it to death!
in a red-yellow rainbow of spray-paint.

I,
I,
I,

doin' it,
doin' it,
doin' it,

to death,
to death,
to death.

I am waiting for the F train.
My womb throbs
when the train thunders.
The smoke-stench fills my nostrils.
I am on my way home from the city
late at night, in a station
where there is probably nothing
to be afraid of.

there is a notion of strength
that is without impact

energy that is still   like water
energy that keeps going   like water
energy that is sustained motion   like water:

turbulence and falls
flats   deeps

and slow dark passages

go down to the water and look

go down to the water and look

go down to the water and look

go down to the water and look

go down to the water and look

1975

Blood

for Kate

You mix flesh, your first time with his paintbox:
raw sienna, white, indian red.
His knife spreads grease rainbows on the palette.
What will you do, now that your father's dead–

you of my poems, whose eyes swallow me
whole, like the dark that drank Persephone–
you spread the paint with delicate bloody strokes
on a large redlipped woman you say is me.

You ripened in my blood like a red fruit
until you split the air with your separate breath.
Then I could not protect you from the fathers;
nor can I bear for you now this father's death.

We paint each other large: daughter, mother,
images delivered of each other's dark.
I've drunk the light of your hair. You've swallowed hell
and can survive the ways it wants you back.

1977

Native Tongue

my first language was wet
and merging.
My syllables were not distinct
from hers; our liquid interface
floated my slow vowels
in the infradark
of her hold,

my serious fish face
my belly wth its tendril
registering her depth
charges.

My first language was light
split by white slats
into molten series
buzzing with dust–
light on my dry, new body.

Vaseline,
clean worm on mama's finger
on my vulva
while I lay,   white diaper, white
chenille spread,   legs across the edge
of the big bed.

My first language was food:
thin, warm thread of milk
dull oatmeal in a pewter bowl,
gingerbread–round boys with raisin eyes,
grandma smiling,   standing at the iron stove
with its porcelain cocks and nipples.

The dog's breathing and the dog's dry tongue–
she was and was not a person.
Dirty they said, but told
how she was Celia's
good girl.
Her high bark
sliced thin portions of the cold.
She was my size.

I was smaller than the steep words
around me: tommy gun, stolen,
hitler. Mother is a nurse's
aide, father is an air raid warden
in the dark cellar. His helmet
is white and important.

We are jews. There are bombs,
oil, an icebox, a victory
garden. You can count by twos
in your hand with fat, green seeds.

1980

Susan Sherman

Because Words Do Not Suffice

Your hands like that   The grass   The sun
Your lips like that   The grass   The rain

It was only that it was so green   The smell of it
The rain that coiled around the grass   The sun
that touched its roots

Only to lie there   My nose furrowed deep in it
As if a moment can be left   The smell of it deep
in the muscles   In the veins

And underneath   As the nostril quivers   lost in the
touch of it   Because we feel the loss of it
Because we feel the death of it

That too much rain will drown the grass
That too much sun will dry the rain
That only in moments is love possible

1962

Lilith of the Wildwood, of the Fair Places

And Lilith left Adam and went to seek her own place
And the gates were closed behind her and her name
was stricken from the Book of Life

1.
And how does one begin again

(Each time, each poem, each line, word, syllable
Each motion of the arms, the legs
a new beginning)

women women surround me
images of women their faces
I who for years pretended them away

pretended away their names their faces
myself what I am pretended it away

as a name exists to confine to define confine
define woman the name the word the definition
the meaning beyond the word the prism prison
beyond the word

to pretend it away

2.
Its the things we feel most
we never say for fear perhaps
that by saying them the things we care most
for will vanish
Love is most like that is the
unsaid thing behind the things we do
when we care most

3.
to be an outcast an outlaw
to stand apart from the law the words
of the law

outlaw

outcast

cast out   cast out by her own will
refusing anything but her own place
a place apart from any other
her own

I do not have to read her legend in the ancient books
I do not have to read their lies
She is here inside me
I reach to touch her

my body my breath my life

4.

To fear you	is to fear myself
To hate you	is to hate myself
To desire you	is to desire myself
To love you	is to love myself

Lilith of the Wildwood
Lilith of the Fair Places

who eats her own children
who is cursed of God

Mother of us all

1971

Love Poem/For A Capricorn

With a hole in my stomach with four grey hairs with a
callus on my toe with 32 years with 32 years
With a record player 53 albums desks and drawers and
shelves of books rooms of thought I come to you
I come as water I come as rain as light falling great
distances I come to you
I come to you in sleep as you walk as time
As tides form as illusion I come to you as night
as sea
I come to you with death inside me with the pain of
death inside me with what it means to leave
I come to you with nothing blind mute I come to you
As laughter I come to you as myself as hair hands eyes
sex I come to you
In madness in love I come to you in minutes hours seconds
in walking running swimming crawling flying
With a dirty apartment I come to you with an empty
refrigerator with a house full of cats
I come to you as water comes to earth as the sea reaches
toward the sand
As lover as friend I come to you as necessity as need

1971

Amerika

1.
How it comes
in answer
to a question
a way of being
included in
of acting on

The fear of losing what we have
holds us immobile
The fear of losing what someday
we think
we might get
keeps us from change

The real illusion
that we possess
anything
that anything possesses us
outside ourselves
our enemies
The gun held to our head

We are betrayed by objects
betray others ourselves
through fear of loss

& lose everything

Amerika you run through our veins
like oil a surface slick
dissolving everything that breathes
that gives
life
There is nothing I regret
but what has gone undone
Amerika this is your fever
your virus
This fear

2.
For 35 years I have fought you
Inside/outside myself
your subtleties   your exaggerations
This lie that bore me
That I refuse to bear
What does it take to communicate
to make people understand
words seldom do it
                    unless they cut
     beneath the surface
go down to the level where pain
begins   where all things give
birth
     Our fear is lost only
in that struggle
In the actions/words of those
who by refusing
               gain

What does it mean to communicate
to understand

3.
I break the surface
grasp for air
It is eight o'clock in the evening
a cold spring night
My anger buoys me past
the surface
          holds me
I gasp for life

Amerika   it is by choice
you are undone
               the courage to name things
To judge

By Terry Turgeon, Ellen Grusse and Jill Raymond
the women in New Haven and Kentucky
who refuse to speak

By Assata Shakur
warrior
and Sam Melville executed
in a prison yard at Attica
By Lolita
Lebron, Diana Oughton and Susan Saxe

Your enemies are endless Amerika
Their very names a poem
Be warned Amerika
your agents spies and friends

By our life we will finally
destroy you
Even as you try to level us
with your death

1975

Terry Turgeon, Ellen Grusse, and Jill Raymond—jailed for refusing to give information to a Grand Jury investigating the women's movement.
Assata Shakur—a Black revolutionary framed on a charge of shooting a policeman in New Jersey, liberated from Clinton Correctional Facility for Women, November 2, 1979.
Sam Melville—a political activist, one of the prisoners executed during the Attica rebellion.
Lolita Lebron—a fighter for Puerto Rican independence, recently freed from Alderson Prison after serving more than twenty years.
Diana Oughton—a member of the Weather Underground, killed when the building she was in was blown up.
Susan Saxe—a lesbian-feminist, currently serving a ten-year sentence in prison as a direct result of politically-motivated acts.

—*S. S.*

Paula Gunn Allen

Madonna of the Hills

She kept finding arrowheads
when she walked to Flower Mountain
and shards of ancient pottery
drawn with brown and black designs—
cloud ladders, lightning stairs and rainbirds.

One day
she took a shovel when she walked that way
and unburied fist-axes, manos, scrapers,
stone knives and some human bones,
which she kept in her collection
on display in her garden.

She said that it gave her
a sense of peace to dig and remember
the women who had cooked and scrubbed
and yelled at their husbands
just like her. She liked, she said,
to go to the spot where she'd found
those things and remember the women
buried there.

It was restful, she said,
and she needed rest—
from her husband's quiet alcohol
and her son who walked around dead.

1965

manos—hand-held grinding stones.
—*P. G. A.*

Wool Season

In Cubero
days too hot, arroyo dry
dust marks the road that forever crumbles at the edge

it will rain next month. Now
time to get the wool in—weighed, paid up, settled,
like in the good times when wool sold by the tons,
even out of Cubero.
Now it's petroleum all the way, and the arroyo gets deeper,
the road narrows a little every year.
Old Diego died in the bottom of the arroyo
a couple of years ago. They say he was drunk,
missed his way in the dark. They found him in the morning.
The old huge boulders I climbed have shattered or moved downstream
in summer floods. The heavy hum of fat flies is the same.

What do the people do when they can't sell their wool?
How do they settle for the lard and mutton and flour?
The kids' clothes, the ladies' shawls, the shovels,
the tires, the gas?
The wool lies heavy in the barn now, season after season,
unsold, unwanted. No one even tans the hides.
They can't survive much more. Being punished for no crimes.
The skin of my thought is bloody wool, stuffed
with gorging ticks like the packed sacks of fleece.

Don't play in the barn where the wool is stacked
they used to warn us kids,
you'll be killed whether you've murdered anyone or not.

1972

Riding the Thunder

1.
Waves rise. The sidewalk talks.
Misunderstood, it recedes—systole,
diastole. History rides my shoulders like a dying falcon,
eyes darting for the surest kill.
President Jackson died of a disease that caused the flesh
to fall off his bones (the Glory of America)
they tied it on with strips of white cloth,
making him presentable for Atlantic kings, his secret lovers.
History's darling, he marched thousands of people hundreds
of miles in celebration of his triumphant will: did

the kings applaud? He achieved honors for this supreme
deliberation, President of the People: the
ancestral graves of the Cherokee made fit homes
for kings, the bodies rotting on the trail
made fine food
for a falcon
Five-sided forms weave around me, I breathe
them in and out. They are the flesh of the people
that I shrink from, wrap my clothing tight around me
pull my thought closer to my bones, oh
do not break my will.
My steps are tides: one
universe at a time takes its five-sided fall
from my body, where thunder lives, hidden.
If I knew what makes me
human I would run in terror to the pools of time
and ride the tides until within/thunder
and my spirit would be one.

2.
In legend told
by smoky fires
where nostrils filled with heat of bodies
full on grease-slick stew (taste
of corn bud lingering on the flesh)
they told of those who rode the thunder long ago
and fell beneath the waves
and on their voices rode the visions
of darkness and no time
the cold center of the lightless wave
the spilled flesh so carefully peeled from bones
possessed, arisen, gone beyond the tales and time:
in legend the dead bring healing to rotted flesh
(see how my hand lies heavy on the air)
where living breath moves unseen clouds
where heaving history falls
far behind, where those who met the thunder and the tide
forever ride.

3.
Climb the spruce tree and dance on the tip
climb into the moutain when it opens for you
follow the winding corridors of winter's tales

enter into the moving paths of shape and time
on an eight-legged horse of blue flame arise:
they will not send you back.
Know the silence of dust, the ache of alone,
the sun will stop just two feet from your door.
The center of time will not turn in the space of now
noon, history, night are
stars, are fixed and counted nails
on the doors of hope, the dying bloody dream.

1974

Andrew Jackson was responsible for the Indian Removal Act that forcibly removed the "Five Civilized Tribes" from the Southeast United States to Oklahoma, then Indian territory. At least one-third of the population died on the march.

–P.G.A.

Creation Story

Light.
Stage of dawn.
Opening on new worlds
for the fourth time.
And not until they came forth
the Fourth Time was it ripe.
That dawn She came,
riding the sun,
humpback flute player heralding Her dawn
the Corn, sweet maiden, riding
the new day
latest in a series
of alternate paths
time of colors
rising.
And the sign of those days would be *4*
She decreed, and the people arising
agreed. So we emerged into consciousness.
Born below in the place of nourishment
where those who have gone
wait, work, and come four days at a time
bringing the rain, coming home.
They fall on the gentle earth, sighing,
the squash, bean, corn sing of growing

and of grace. Pollen on the air golden
in that time, glowing, that return.
So on that day was given all this,
called Iyetico, called Mother,
the clans, the people, the deer:
tracks left here and there
are signs.

1977

4—The number 4 is held to be the sacred earth number among many American Indian peoples, including the Laguna Pueblos to whom the story told in the poem belongs.
Iyetico (ee-yeh-tih-co)—also referred to as *ya-ya* (mother). She is the equivalent of the Earth Goddess (not to be confused with the Supreme Being who is known at Laguna as *Ts'its'tsi'nako* (Thought Woman).

—*P. G. A.*

Powwow '79, Durango

haven't been to one in almost three years
there's six drums and 200 dancers a few
booths piled with jewelry and powwow stuff
some pottery and oven bread
everyone gathers
stands for the grand entry
two flag songs
and the opening prayer by some guy
works for the BIA
who asks our father
to bless our cars
to heal our hearts
to let the music here tonight
make us better, cool
hurts and unease
in his son's name, amen.
my daughter arrives, stoned,
brown face ashy from the weed,
there's no toilet paper
in the *ladies* room she accuses me
there's never any toilet paper
in the ladies room at a powwow she glares
changes
calms

it's like being home after a long time
are you gonna dance I ask
here's my shawl
not dressed right she says
the new beaded ties I bought her swing
from her long dark braids
why not you have dark blue on I say
look.
we step inside the gym
eyes sweep the rubber floor
jackets, jeans, down-filled vests,
sweatshirts all dark blue.
have to look close to pick out
occasional brown or red on older folks
the dark brown faces rising on the bleachers
the dark hair on almost every head
ever see so many Indians
you're dressed right
we look at the bleachers
quiet like shadows
the people sit watching the floor below
where dancers circle the beating drums
exploding color in the light.

1979

BIA—Bureau of Indian Affairs, a U.S. government agency.
Blue—large numbers of modern Indian people prefer to wear dark-blue jackets and jeans in the West.

—P.G.A.

Beloved Women

It is not known if those
who warred and hunted on the plains
chanted and hexed in the hills
divined and healed in the mountains
gazed and walked beneath the seas
were Lesbians
It is never known
if any woman was a Lesbian
so who can say that
she who shivering drank

warm blood beneath wind-blown moons
slept tight to a beloved of shininghair
curled as a smile within crescent arms
followed her track deep into secret woods
dreamed other dreams
and who would record these things
perhaps all women are
Lesbian though many try
to turn knotted sinew and stubby cheek
into that ancient almostremembered scene
perhaps all know the first
beloved so well
they can shape the power
to reclaim her

The portents in the skies–
the moons forever growing and falling
away, the suns concentric orbits
daily crossing themselves like a nun–
who's to say that these are signs
of what has always been?
And perhaps the portents are better
left written only in the stars,
etched on cave-walls, rosewindows,
the perfect naves of brooding
cathedrals. Perhaps
all they signify is best left
unsaid.

Nobody knows whether those women
were Lesbians. Nobody
can say what such an event
might mean.

1980

Judy Grahn

from The Common Woman Poems

2. Ella, in a square apron, along Highway 80

She's a copperheaded waitress,
tired and sharp-worded, she hides
her bad brown tooth behind a wicked
smile, and flicks her ass
out of habit, to fend off the pass
that passes for affection.
She keeps her mind the way men
keep a knife–keen to strip the game
down to her size. She has a thin spine,
swallows her eggs cold, and tells lies.
She slaps a wet rag at the truck drivers
if they should complain. She understands
the necessity for pain, turns away
the smaller tips, out of pride, and
keeps a flask under the counter. Once,
she shot a lover who misused her child.
Before she got out of jail, the courts had pounced
and given the child away. Like some isolated lake,
her flat blue eyes take care of their own stark
bottoms. Her hands are nervous, curled, ready
to scrape.
The common woman is as common
as a rattlesnake.

4. Carol, in the park, chewing on straws

She has taken a woman lover
whatever shall we do
she has taken a woman lover
how lucky it wasnt you
And all the day through she smiles and lies
and grits her teeth and pretends to be shy,
or weak, or busy. Then she goes home
and pounds her own nails, makes her own
bets, and fixes her own car, with her friend.
She goes as far
as women can go without protection
from men.

On weekends, she dreams of becoming a tree;
a tree that dreams it is ground up
and sent to the paper factory, where it
lies helpless in sheets, until it dreams
of becoming a paper airplane, and rises
on its own current; where it turns into a
bird, a great coasting bird that dreams of becoming
more free, even, than that—a feather, finally, or
a piece of air with lightning in it.
    she has taken a woman lover
    whatever can we say
She walks around all day
quietly, but underneath it
she's electric;
angry energy inside a passive form.
The common woman is as common
as a thunderstorm.

7. Vera, from my childhood

Solemnly swearing, to swear as an oath to you
who have somehow gotten to be a pale old woman;
swearing, as if an oath could be wrapped around
your shoulders
like a new coat:
For your 28 dollars a week and the bastard boss
you never let yourself hate;
and the work, all the work you did at home
where you never got paid;
For your mouth that got thinner and thinner
until it disappeared as if you had choked on it,
watching the hard liquor break your fine husband down
into a dead joke.
For the strange mole, like a third eye
right in the middle of your forehead;
for your religion which insisted that people
are beautiful golden birds and must be preserved;
for your persistent nerve
and plain white talk—
the common woman is as common
as good bread
as common as when you couldnt go on
but did.

For all the world we didnt know we held in common
all along
the common woman is as common as the best of bread
and will rise
and will become strong—I swear it to you
I swear it to you on my own head
I swear it to you on my common
woman's
head

1969

A History of Lesbianism

How they came into the world,
the women-loving-women
came in three by three
and four by four
the women-loving-women
came in ten by ten
and ten by ten again
until there were more
than you could count

they took care of each other
the best they knew how
and of each other's children,
if they had any.

How they lived in the world,
the women-loving-women
learned as much as they were allowed
and walked and wore their clothes
the way they liked
whenever they could. They did whatever
they knew to be happy or free
and worked and worked and worked.
The women-loving-women
in America were called dykes
and some liked it
and some did not.

they made love to each other
the best they knew how
and for the best reasons

How they went out of the world,
the women-loving-women
went out one by one
having withstood greater and lesser
trials, and much hatred
from other people, they went out
one by one, each having tried
in her own way to overthrow
the rule of men over women,
they tried it one by one
and hundred by hundred,
until each came in her own way
to the end of her life
and died.

The subject of lesbianism
is very ordinary; it's the question
of male domination that makes everybody
angry.

1970

I am the wall at the lip of the water
I am the rock that refused to be battered
I am the dyke in the matter, the other
I am the wall with the womanly swagger
I am the dragon, the dangerous dagger
I am the bulldyke, the bulldagger

and I have been many a wicked grandmother
and I shall be many a wicked daughter.

1972

the woman whose head is on fire
the woman with a noisy voice
the woman with too many fingers
the woman who never smiled once in her life
the woman with a boney body
the woman with moles all over her

the woman who cut off her breast
the woman with a large bobbing head
the woman with one glass eye
the woman with broad shoulders
the woman with callused elbows
the woman with a sunken chest
the woman who is part giraffe

the woman with five gold teeth
the woman who looks straight ahead
the woman with enormous knees
the woman who can lick her own clitoris
the woman who screams on the trumpet
the woman whose toes grew together
the woman who says I am what I am

the woman with rice under her skin
the woman who owns a machete
the woman who plants potatoes
the woman who murders the kangaroo
the woman who stuffs clothing into a sack
the woman who makes a great racket
the woman who fixes machines
the woman whose chin is sticking out
the woman who says I will be

the woman who carries laundry on her head
the woman who is part horse
the woman who asks so many questions
the woman who cut somebody's throat

the woman who gathers peaches
the woman who carries jars on her head
the woman who howls
the woman whose nose is broken
the woman who constructs buildings

the woman who has fits on the floor
the woman who makes rain happen
the woman who refuses to menstruate

the woman who sets broken bones
the woman who sleeps out on the street
the woman who plays the drums
the woman who is part grasshopper
the woman who herds cattle
the woman whose will is unbending
the woman who hates kittens

the woman who escaped from the jailhouse
the woman who is walking across the desert
the woman who buries the dead
the woman who taught herself writing
the woman who skins rabbits
the woman who believes her own word
the woman who chews bearskin
the woman who eats cocaine
the woman who thinks about everything

the woman who has the tattoo of a bird
the woman who puts things together
the woman who squats on her haunches
the woman whose children are all different colors

singing   i am the will of the woman
                           the woman
                           my will is unbending

when She-Who-moves-the-earth will turn over
when She Who moves, the earth will turn over.

1972

She Who continues.
She Who has a being
named She Who is a being
named She Who carries her own name.
She Who turns things over.
She Who marks her own way, gathering.
She Who makes her own difference.
She Who differs, gathering her own events.

She Who gathers, gaining
She Who carries her own ways,
gathering She Who waits,
bearing She Who cares for her
own name, carrying She Who
bears, gathering She Who cares
for She Who gathers her own ways,
carrying
the names of She Who gather and gain,

singing I am the woman, the woman
the woman—I am the first person.

and the first person is She Who is the first
person to She Who is the first person to no
other. There is no other first person.

She Who floods like a river and
like a river continues
She Who continues

1972

from A Woman Is Talking to Death

2.
They don't have to lynch the women anymore

death sits on my doorstep
cleaning his revolver

death cripples my feet and sends me out
to wait for the bus alone,
then comes by driving a taxi.

the woman on our block with 6 young children
has the most vacant of eyes
death sits in her bedroom, loading
his revolver

they don't have to lynch the women
very often anymore, although
they used to–the lord and his men
went through the villages at night, beating &
killing every woman caught
outdoors.
the European witch trials took away
the independent people; two different villages
—after the trials were through that year—
had left in them, each—
one living woman:
one

What were those other women up to? had they
run over someone? stopped on the wrong bridge?
did they have teeth like
any kind of geese, or children
in them?

3.
This woman is a lesbian be careful

In the military hospital where I worked
as a nurse's aide, the walls of the halls
were lined with howling women
waiting to deliver
or to have some parts removed.
One of the big private rooms contained
the general's wife, who needed
a wart taken off her nose.
we were instructed to give her special attention
not because of her wart or her nose
but because of her husband, the general.

as many women as men die, and that's a fact.

At work there was one friendly patient, already

claimed, a young woman burnt apart with X-ray,
she had long white tubes instead of openings;
rectum, bladder, vagina–I combed her hair, it
was my job, but she took care of me as if
nobody's touch could spoil her.

ho ho death, ho death
have you seen the twinkle in the dead woman's eye?

when you are a nurse's aide
someone suddenly notices you
and yells about the patient's bed,
and tears the sheets apart so you
can do it over, and over
while the patient waits
doubled over in her pain
for you to make the bed *again*
and no one ever looks at you,
only at what you do not do

Here, general, hold this soldier's bed pan
for a moment, hold it for a year–
then we'll promote you to making his bed.
we believe you wouldn't make such messes
if you had to clean up after them.

that's a fantasy.
this woman is a lesbian, be careful.

When I was arrested and being thrown out
of the military, the order went out: don't anybody
speak to this woman, and for those three
long months, almost nobody did; the dayroom, when
I entered it, fell silent til I had gone; they
were afraid, they knew the wind would blow
them over the rail, the cops would come,
the water would run into their lungs.
Everything I touched
was spoiled. They were my lovers, those
women, but nobody had taught us to swim.
I drowned, I took 3 or 4 others down
when I signed the confession of what we
had done together.

No one will ever speak to me again.

I read this somewhere; I wasn't there:
in WW II the US army had invented some floating
amphibian tanks, and took them over to
the coast of Europe to unload them,
the landing ships all drawn up in a fleet,
and everybody watching. Each tank had a
crew of 6 and there were 25 tanks.
The first went down the landing planks
and sank, the second, the third, the
fourth, the fifth, the sixth went down
and sank. They weren't supposed
to sink, the engineers had
made a mistake. The crews looked around
wildly for the order to quit,
but none came, and in the sight of
thousands of men, each 6 crewmen
saluted his officers, battened down
his hatch in turn and drove into the
sea, and drowned, until all 25 tanks
were gone. did they have vacant
eyes, die laughing, or what? what
did they talk about, those men,
as the water came in?

was the general their lover?

4. A Mock Interrogation
Have you ever held hands with a woman?

Yes, many times—women about to deliver, women about to have breasts removed, wombs removed, miscarriages, women having epileptic fits, having asthma, cancer, women having breast bone marrow sucked out of them by nervous or indifferent interns, women with heart condition, who were vomiting, overdosed, depressed, drunk, lonely to the point of extinction: women who had been run over, beaten up. deserted. starved. women who had been bitten by rats; and women who were happy, who were celebrating, who were dancing with me in large circles or alone, women who were climbing mountains or up and down walls, or trucks or roofs and needed a boost up, or I did; women who simply wanted to hold my hand because they liked me, some women who wanted to hold my hand because they liked me better than anyone.

These were many women?

Yes. Many.

What about kissing? Have you kissed any women?

I have kissed many women.

When was the first woman you kissed with serious feeling?

The first woman ever I kissed was Josie, who I had loved at such a distance for months. Josie was not only beautiful, she was tough and handsome too. Josie had black hair and white teeth and strong brown muscles. Then she dropped out of school unexplained. When she came back she came back for one day only, to finish the term, and there was a child in her. She was all shame, pain, and defiance. Her eyes were dark as the water under a bridge and no one would talk to her, they laughed and threw things at her. In the afternoon I walked across the front of the class and looked deep into Josie's eyes and I picked up her chin with my hand, because I loved her, because nothing like her trouble would ever happen to me, because I hated it that she was pregnant and unhappy, and an outcast. We were thirteen.

You didn't kiss her?

How does it feel to be thirteen and having a baby?

You didn't actually kiss her?

Not in fact.

You have kissed other women?

Yes, many, some of the finest women I know, I have kissed. women who were lonely, women I didn't know and didn't want to, but kissed because that was a way to say yes we are still alive and loveable, though separate, women who recognized a loneliness in me, women who were hurt, I confess to kissing the top of a 55 year old woman's head in the snow in boston, who was hurt more deeply than I have ever been hurt, and I wanted her as a very few people have wanted me–I wanted her and me to own and control and run the city we lived in, to staff the hospital I knew would mistreat her, to drive the transportation system that had betrayed her, to patrol the streets controlling the men who would murder or disfigure or disrupt us, not accidentally with machines, but on purpose because we are not allowed out on the street alone–

Have you ever committed any indecent acts with women?

Yes, many. I am guilty of allowing suicidal women to die before my eyes or in my ears or under my hands because I thought I could do nothing, I am guilty of leaving a prostitute who held a knife to my friend's throat to keep us from leaving, because we would not sleep with her, we thought she was old and fat and ugly; I am guilty of not loving her who needed me; I regret all the women I have not slept with or comforted, who pulled themselves away from me for lack of something I had not the courage to fight for, for us, our life, our planet, our city, our meat and potatoes, our love. These are indecent acts, lacking courage, lacking a certain fire behind the eyes, which is the symbol, the raised fist, the sharing of resources, the resistance that tells death he will starve for lack of the fat of us, our extra. Yes I have committed acts of indecency with women and most of them were acts of omission. I regret them bitterly.

7. Death and Disfiguration

One Christmas eve my lovers and I
we left the bar, driving home slow
there was a woman lying in the snow
by the side of the road. She was wearing
a bathrobe and no shoes, where were
her shoes? she had turned the snow
pink, under her feet. she was an Asian
woman, didn't speak much English, but
she said a taxi driver beat her up
and raped her, throwing her out of his
care.
what on earth was she doing there
on a street she helped to pay for
but doesn't own?
doesn't she know to stay home?

I am a pervert, therefore I've learned
to keep my hands to myself in public
but I was so drunk that night,
I actually did something loving.
I took her in my arms, this woman,
until she could breathe right, and
my friends who are perverts too
they touched her too
we all touched her.
"You're going to be all right"

we lied. She started to cry.
"I'm 55 years old" she said
and that said everything.

Six big policemen answered the call
no child *in* them.
they seemed afraid to touch her,
then grabbed her like a corpse and heaved her
on their metal stretcher into the van,
crashing and clumsy.
She was more frightened than before.
they were cold and bored.
"don't leave me" she said.
"she'll be all right" they said.
we left, as we have left all of our lovers
as all lovers leave all lovers
much too soon to get the real loving done.

9.
Hey you death

ho and ho poor death
our lovers teeth are white geese flying above us
our lovers muscles are rope ladders under our hands
even though no women yet go down to the sea in ships
except in their dreams.

only the arrogant invent a quick and meaningful end
for themselves, of their own choosing.
everyone else knows how very slow it happens
how the woman's existence bleeds out her years,
how the child shoots up at ten and is arrested and old
how the man carries a murderous shell within him
and passes it on.

we are the fat of the land, and
we all have our list of casualties

to my lovers I bequeath
the rest of my life

I want nothing left of me for you, ho death
except some fertilizer
for the next batch of us

who do not hold hands with you
who do not embrace you
who try not to work for you
or sacrifice themselves or trust
or believe you, ho ignorant
death, how do you know
we happened to you?

wherever our meat hangs on our bones
for our own use
your pot is so empty
death, ho death
you shall be poor

1973

A Funeral
Plainsong from a Younger Woman to an Older Woman

i will be your mouth now, to do your singing
breath belongs to those who do the breathing.
warm life, as it passes through your fingers
flares up in the very hands you will be leaving

you have left, what is left
for the bond between women is a circle
we are together within it.

i am your best, i am your kind
kind of my kind, i am your wish
wish of my wish, i am your breast
breast of my breast, i am your mind
mind of my mind, i am your flesh
i am your kind, i am your wish
kind of my kind, i am your best

now you have left you can be
wherever the fire is when it blows itself out.
now you are a voice in any wind
        i am a single wind
now you are any source of a fire
        i am a single fire

wherever you go to, i will arrive
whatever i have been, you will come back to
wherever you leave off, i will inherit
whatever i resurrect, you shall have it

you have right, what is right
for the bond between women is returning
we are endlessly within it
and endlessly apart within it.
it is not finished
it will not be finished

i will be your heart now, to do your loving
love belongs to those who do the feeling.

life, as it stands so still along your fingers
beats in my hands, the hands i will, believing
that you have become she, who is not, any longer
somewhere in particular

we are together in your stillness
you have wished us a bonded life

love of my love, i am your breast
arm of my arm, i am your strength
breath of my breath, i am your foot
thigh of my thigh, back of my back
eye of my eye, beat of my beat
kind of my kind, i am your best

when you were dead i said you had gone to the mountain

the trees do not yet speak of you

a mountain when it is no longer
a mountain, goes to the sea
when the sea dies it goes to the rain
when the rain dies it goes to the grain
when the grain dies it goes to the flesh
when the flesh dies it goes to the mountain

now you have left, you can wander
will you tell whoever could listen

tell all the voices who speak to younger women
tell all the voices who speak to us when we need it
that the love between women is a circle
and is not finished

wherever i go to, you will arrive
whatever you have been, i will come back to
wherever i leave off, you will inherit
whatever we resurrect, we shall have it
we shall have it, we have right

and you have left, what is left

i will take your part now, to do your daring
lots belong to those who do the sharing.
i will be your fight now, to do your winning
as the bond between women is beginning
in the middle at the end
my first beloved, present friend
if i could die like the next rain
i'd call you by your mountain name
and rain on you

want of my want, i am your lust
wave of my wave, i am your crest
earth of my earth, i am your crust
may of my may, i am your must
kind of my kind, i am your best

tallest mountain least mouse
least mountain tallest mouse

you have put your very breath upon mine
i shall wrap my entire fist around you
i can touch any woman's lip to remember

we are together in my motion
you have wished us a bonded life

a funeral: for my first lover and longtime friend
Yvonne Mary Robinson b. Oct. 20, 1939; d. Nov. 1974
for ritual use only

1974

Irena Klepfisz

death camp

when they took us   to the shower   i saw
the rebbitzin   her sagging breasts   sparse
pubic hairs   i knew   and remembered
the old rebbe   and turned   my eyes away
i could still hear   her advice   a woman
with a husband   a scholar

when they turned   on the gas   i smelled
it   first   coming at me   pressed myself
hard to the wall   crying   rebbitzin   rebbitzin
i am here with you   and the advice you gave me
i screamed   into the wall   as the blood burst from
my lungs   cracking   her nails in women's flesh   i watched
her capsize   beneath me   my blood in her mouth   i screamed

when they dragged my body   into the oven   i burned
slowly at first   i could smell my own flesh   and could
hear   them grunt   with the weight of the rebbitzin
and they flung   her on top   of me   and i could smell
her hair burning   against my stomach

when i pressed through   the chimney
it was sunny   and clear   my smoke
was distinct   i rose quiet   left her
beneath

1973

Rebbitzin (Yiddish)—rabbi's wife.
Rebbe—rabbi.

they're always curious

they're always curious about what you eat as if you were
some strange breed still unclassified by darwin & whether
you cook every night & wouldn't it be easier for you to
buy frozen dinners but i am quick to point out that my intra-
venous tubing has been taken out & they back up saying *i*

could never just cook for one person but i tell them it's
the same exactly the same as for two except half

but more they're curious about what you do when the urge
is on & if you use a coke bottle or some psychedelic dildo
or electric vibrator or just the good old finger or whole
hand & do you mannippppulllaaatttte yourself into a clit
orgasm or just kind of keep digging away at yourself & if
you mind it & when you have affairs doesn't it hurt when it's
over & it certainly must be lonely to go back to the old finger

& they always cluck over the amount of space you require
& certainly the extra bedroom seems unnecessary & i try to
explain that i like to move around & that i get antsy when
i have the urge so that it's nice to have an extra place
to go when you're lonely & after all it seems small compen-
sation for using the good old finger & they're surprised be-
cause they never thought of it that way & it does seem reason-
able come to think of it

& they kind of probe about your future & if you have a will or
why you bother to accumulate all that stuff or what you plan
to do with your old age & aren't you scared about being put
away somewhere or found on your bathroom floor dead after
your downstairs neighbor has smelled you out but then of course
you don't have the worry of who goes first though of course
you know couples live longer for they have something to live
for & i try to explain i live for myself even when in love but
it's a hard concept to explain when you feel lonely

1974

they did not build wings for them

they did not build wings for them
the unmarried aunts;   instead they
crammed them into old maids' rooms
or placed them as nannies with
the younger children;   mostly they
ate in the kitchen, but sometimes
were permitted to dine with the family
for which they were grateful and
smiled graciously as the food was passed.

they would eat slowly never filling
their plates and their hearts would
sink at the evening's end when it was
time to retreat into an upstairs corner.

but there were some who did not smile
who never wished to be grafted on
the bursting houses. these few remained
indifferent to the family gatherings
preferring the aloneness of their small rooms
which they decorated with odd objects
found on long walks. they collected
bird feathers and skulls unafraid to clean
them to whiteness; stones which resembled
humped bears or the more common tiger and
wolf; dried leaves whose brilliant colors
never faded; pieces of wood still covered
with fresh moss and earth which retained
their moisture and continued flourishing.
these they placed by their dresser mirror
in arrangements reminiscent of secret rites
or hung over delicate watercolors of unruly
trees whose branches were about to snap
with the wind.

it happened sometimes that among these
one would venture even further. periodically
would be heard vague tales of a woman
withdrawn and inaccessible suddenly disappearing
one autumn night leaving her room bare
of herself. women gossiped about a man.
but eventually word would come back
she had moved north to the ocean and lived
alone. she was still collecting
but now her house was filled with crab
and lobster shells; discolored claws
which looked like grinning south american
parrots trapped in fish nets decorated
the walls; skulls of unidentifiable
creatures were arranged in geometric patterns
and soft reeds in tall green bottles
lined the window sills. one room
in the back with totally bare walls

was a workshop. here she sorted colored
shells and pasted them on wooden boards
in the shape of common flowers. these she sold
without sentiment.

such a one might also disappear inland.
rumor would claim she had travelled in
men's clothing. two years later it would
be reported she had settled in the woods
on some cleared land. she ran a small farm
mainly for supplying herself with food
and wore strangely patched dresses and shawls
of oddly matched materials. but aloneness
was her real distinction. the house was neat
and the pantry full. seascapes and pastoral
scenes hung on the walls. the garden was
well kept and the flower beds clearly defined
by color: red yellow blue. in the woods
five miles from the house she had an orchard.
here she secretly grafted and crossed varieties
creating singular fruit of shades and scents
never thought possible. her experiments rarely
failed and each spring she waited eagerly to see
what new forms would hang from the trees.
here the world was a passionate place and she
would visit it at night baring her breasts
to the moon.

1974

from The Monkey House and Other Cages

(The voice is that of a female monkey born and raised in a zoo.)

1.
to state each horror
would be redundant. the objects
themselves suffice: a broken comb
an umbrella handle a piece of blue
plastic chipped pocket mirror.

the face is unfriendly.
i try to outstare it but
it persists moving

spastically   the eyes
twitching open shut
nose quivering wrinkled fingers
picking at the ears. i do not know

this stranger.

2.
i have heard of tortures
yet remain
strangely safe.
                  but at night
i am torn by my own
dreams see myself live
the grossest indignities probes

and unable to rip myself from my flesh
i remain silent not
uttering sound nor moan not
bothering to feel pain.

waking in early light
alone untouched
i cry over my safety.

3.
when they first come
they screech with wildness
flinging themselves against the wall
and then against the bars.

some sit and cry for days
some never recover and
die.
        they are familiar
yet crap uncontrollably plead
shiver and rock. i refuse

to have anything to do with them
till they learn to behave.

4.
at her arrival   she was
stunned and bruised.   she
folded up   refusing to eat

her mouth grim.   i staked
out my territory   recognizing
her fierceness   her strength.

but she weakened   grew sick
was removed without resistance
returned three days later
shaved patches on her arms.

later she told me: we create
the responses around us.

5.
i remember the grasp of her claws
the vicious bite   the scar
still on my leg.   she was crazed

jabbering   then attacking
again.   and the sun seemed to fall away
into coldness   as i pressed myself
against the corner   the hardened sand
under my nails.   i began to gnaw
through concrete   my face raw.

they took her away
and when she came back
she did not look at me.

6.
scatter yourself
i told her   moving
myself into the left
corner   where i sat
observing the movement
of her head.

she nodded

seemed to sleep
then stood up   pointing
outside.   the leaves were
red.   it was a falling time
noisy   dry twigs cracking
off nearby trees.   i felt

content   watching myself
while she pointed   the leaves
red.

7.

and finally
she said   this is enough
and began to bang her head
against the wall   one thud

after another thud   she batted
herself beginning to bleed
throwing herself and falling.

they came   and tried to seize
her   while the sun vanished
and the trees moved slowly

and everyone   so still
afraid to breathe: the moon
all fresh   and the birds
small balls of feathers.

i puked as they dragged her out:
tufts of fur on the stone floor.

8.
when she died   i mourned
a silent mourning.

and
the others asked
asked   asked
and poked at me.

there had been much between us
in gesture. mostly i remember
her yellowed teeth her attempt
at tameness.

9.
there had been no sound:
just the motion of our hands
our lips sucked in
toes pointed outward.
it had been enough.

dizzy
with messages i would lie
down dream of different
enclosures.

1975-1976

Contexts

for Tillie Olsen

Dollars damn me.
—Herman Melville, as cited in *Silences.*

I have no patience with this dreadful idea that whatever you have in you has to come out, that you can't suppress true talent. People can be destroyed; they can be bent, distorted, and completely crippled.
—Katherine Anne Porter, *ibid.*

1.
I am helping proofread the history
of a dead language. I read out loud
to an old man whose eyes have failed
him. He no longer sees the difference
between a period or a comma, a dash
or a hyphen, and needs me for I under-
stand how important these distinctions are.

The room is crammed with books, books
he had systematically tagged for future
projects—now lost. Sounds pour out

of me. I try to inject some feeling
and focus, concentrate on the meaning
of each linguistic phrase. On the edge
of my vision, he huddles over a blurred
page, moves his magnifying glass from line
to line, and we progress. Time passes.
My voice is a stranger's, sensible and
calm, and I, the cornered, attentive hostess,
listen in silence as it conjectures the his-
tory of languages long dead without a trace.
How, I wonder, did I become what I am not?

I request a break. The sounds cease.
I check the clock, calculate, write
figures in a notebook. I am numb
and stiff, walk up and down the hall,
stare into busy offices. I wait.
I wait for something forgotten, something
caught and bruised: a brown feather,
a shaft of green light, a certain word.
I bend, drink water, remember stubborn
clams clinging to the muddy bottom.

2.
The building across the street
has an ordinary facade, a view of the park
and rows of symmetrical spotless windows.
Each morning, the working women come to perform
their duties. They are in starched white,
could pass for vigilant nurses keeping
order and quiet around those about to die.
And each morning, idle women
in pale blue housecoats, frilled and fluffed
at the edges, stare out of double windows,
waiting for something to begin.

With whom would you change places, I ask
myself, the maid or the mistress?

3.
The clock sucks me back. I calculate the loss,
return to the books, his unrecognizing eyes.

He is unaware of the pantomime outside,
feels no rage that I and the world are lost
to him, only mourns the words dead on the page.
We begin again. I point to the paragraph,
synchronize the movement of the eye and mouth,
abandon all pretense of feeling. Silently I float
out, out toward the horizon, out toward the open sea,
leaving behind the dull drone of an efficient machine.

I am
there again, standing by the railing, watching
the whales in their narrow aquarium, watching
their gleaming grace in the monotonous circle, watching
how they hunger for fleshly contact, how the young keeper
places his human hand in their rough pink mouths,
rubs their tongues, splashes them like babies. I cannot
watch them enough, but feel deeply ashamed for I know
the price.

With a shock I realize we are not together,
that he is lost, caught in a trap.
He sounds the words over and over, moves
the glass back and forth, insists there is
a lapse in meaning. I sit silent, tense, watch
as he painfully untangles the subtle error, watch
as he leans back exhausted saying: "I knew something
was wrong! I knew from the context that something
was wrong!"

4.
At the end of the day I stack the galleys,
mark an *x* where we've been forced to stop.
He is reluctant to let me go, anxious, un-
certain about the coming days, but I smile,
assure him they'll be all the same. Alone,
I rush for the bulb-lit train, for the empty
corner of the crowded car, then begin the struggle
against his sightless eyes, against the memory
of a vacant stare.

It is a story, I tell myself, at least
a story, that one Sunday when I refused
to go to work. Fifteen, bored with inventory
and week-end jobs, I stayed in bed and,
already expert, called in sick. Her rage
was almost savage, wild. She paced
through the apartment, returned to me again
and again saying *"Get up! Get up now!"*
as if I was in mortal danger. But nothing
would move me from my bed, from the sun
cutting through the iron fire escape outside,
from the half-finished book about the man
and the whale. "It's not that much money,"
I called to her.

And then her inexplicable silence. At first
she sat in the kitchen, fingering the piece
of cloth, staring absently at the teacup.
Finally she got up, began pinning the pattern.
Soon I heard the clean sound of the scissor
against the kitchen table, then silence again
as she basted. Much later that day, she worked
on the machine, and still she did not speak
to me, just let the bobbing needle make its own
uninterrupted noise. And as I went to bed
new with the excitement of that sea of words,
filled with my own infinite possibilities, she
continued sewing, fulfilling her obligation
for the next day's fitting.

5.
The blind man balances easily in the rocking
car. He moves among us, sings, shakes a tin
cup. Most of us think it's all a con, but it
makes no difference. Pose is part of necessity.
Riding each evening through the echoing tunnels,
I've begun to believe in the existence of my own
soul, its frailty, its ability to grow narrow,
small. I've begun to understand what it means
to be born mute, to be born without hope of speech.

1980

Rota Silverstrini

Unfinished

Braown–Bom–bo
        with your chocolate skin
        and your spanish tongue
        and your boyish laughter
You return to haunt
the memory of a
friendship formed

Braown–Bom–bo
Your mother's delight

        Didn't our mamas
        sit en la cosina
        with
        el cafe con leche
        y la religion
        as if it were all
        and
        wasn't it all
        just then
                Braown–Bom–bo

Eddie couldn't meet your
mama's standards/
in her blind dead eyes
he disappeared into
death's darkness
dying   dying
at the church steps
where other junkies
entered the mainstream
of la vida americana

at the church steps
his death redeemed him
his OD carried him
to peace / costly peace

Christ walked away
laughing   laughing
at ricans who
worship the
god on the
never arriving dollar

And
when it came, yeah
cuando el peso vino
christ walked with
ricans to suburbs
to forget themselves
with los americanos
who befriended them
in the dollared name of jesus

1975

en la cosina (Spanish)—in the kitchen.
el café con leche—with milk.
y la religion—and religion.
la vida americana—the American life.
cuando el peso vino—when the dollar came.

Pieces of Echoes

1.
I can see the street
from barricaded windows
snow covered streets
footprinted/boots
leave signs
window-ledge-cold
seeps in

She tapped me on my cold shoulders
I shivered slightly
her nurse's uniform
starched to fit
the sterilizing image

I must turn about
   must respond   her
light tap, authoritative

2.
I can see the street
from barricaded windows
can turn my face from
snow covered streets
turn it to dark. brown tiles
cold, so cold beneath my feet
I rest my head   pretend
pretend
I'm in a safe place, now
footprinted streets are
simply images that seep
through cold windows

3.
Nurse Malloy taps me
I've responded too slowly, again
She taps me knowing
I've turned my face
but not my heart
from them cold, wintery streets
She taps me
I can't inject myself
drugs being illegal and
all that
I must serve my arm
instead to nurse Malloy

4.
I wear barricaded woven
pigtails
yellow blue red
red
can't see woolworth's
ribbon counter from
where I stand
can't see anything
I've served my arm, legally
to nurse Malloy

turned turned
from the windows

I'm dressed again
respected
She doesn't tap me, anymore

1976

Martha Courtot

i am a woman in ice
melting

piece by piece
slowly
i am divested
of the cold cage

sharp as glass
the splinters fall at my feet
do not cut yourself

when i listen
to the trains wail
i can feel
through underground caverns
of stalactal promises

the earth
full and steady
under me
move

i never thought
i'd love the sun again
but now my fingers move
in a panic
of wanting to be burnt

1973

Jacqueline Lapidus

Coming Out

the first person I loved
was a woman   my passion
for her lasted thirty years
and was not returned
she never let me suck her nipples
she kept secrets between her legs
she told me men would love me
for myself   she couldn't tell me
ways to love myself
she didn't know

Mother, I would like to help you
swim back against the foaming river
to the source of our
incestuous fears
but you're so tired
out beyond the breakers
and I am upstream among my sisters
spawning

1975

Susan Wood-Thompson

Fever

A girl of six, drenched, throws the covers off.
Her parents, old and country, pack them back
around her. Feebly in the evening she plays
cards with her aunt, waiting for the little
red marks to go.

Hearts and diamonds fade,
tonight she cannot read the cards, tonight
she learns silence, what it looks like forever
behind her head.

Crafty-eared, she hears
her mother cry, head in apron in the kitchen,
crying out the child who has stopped stirring in her,
whose eyes burned out. Crying guilt that has no origin,
no name.

The child knows. Because the old man
used to come and touch her with that thing
inside her pants, inside her brain, to tell
her forever she's a bad girl: Good girls
don't have that happen to them. Good girls don't
go blind.

The child knows God sees everything.

1976

Territory

In the chapel
the floor was linoleum
and the air gorgeous with beeswax.
The sisters' stalls faced the altar
and one afternoon through the window
I had seen them chant and bow in unison
toward the aisle.

The stalls,
with slab drop seats, were old wood
dull with a century of breviaries
resting lightly
the floor dull with heavy shoes
moving softly by.

Here the nuns in secret
who never mentioned religion
came to say what else they believed
who else, besides the sick, they loved;
to try to make sense out of the flat days
in Galveston when the salt wind didn't lift starched veils
when God did not make himself known
when nothing was like growing up in Ireland
in the countryside, holding piglets,
housing and hiding gypsies.

Here I came in secret
barefooted for quiet
to smell the beeswax
to catch the sanctuary fire flickering unseen
to watch the moon whiten the curves of the stalls.
Silent as the pulse pounding
I listened for soft steps and the words
"You do not belong here."

My fingers swiftly handled the breviaries
I peered at the sisters' holy cards, tried each stall
expecting the trap door to hell
to drop open under my knees
for coming in moonlight
believing in fire
for not knowing
my place.

1977

Marilyn Hacker

Up from D.C.

We were six women. My lover
was the youngest. Her cabled shoulders
glistened like her short dark hair.
Tucked, unnoticed, in a sprawling slum
our house was under siege.

We were six women, one
my lover, in a wooden
house, waiting
for the danger
to be over.

In a round tin tub
a woman scrubs
the shape from a baby's
face. The plump brown
child's red hair-ribbon tells: a girl.
Immerses her again, head
under. I cry out, seize her.
You, baby-shaped, face
shapeless, sprawl in a
deck-chair. I run, gasping, grab
you too. Is it too late?
Your chins lump like putty.

We looked out a cracked window
on the second floor, from a bare
room: scorched floor-planks, cobwebs.
Dust. Dusty outside,
porched row-houses of a Southern slum,
one, cater-corner across, enamelled red.
Coffee-cans sprout grapefruit shrubs from pits.
An old Black woman in a faded print
dress sits behind them, rocking,
waiting for the danger to be over.

Her sweaty runner's limbs
sprawl across mine, arm on
my shoulder, calf

knotted against my knee. We hunch
below the windowsill, cramped. Still
heat. Roaches run errands.
Her angular
cheekbones glint like blades.
After this, we will not
scavenge. We hope
to survive. The others move
lightly in the hallway. One bald bulb
dangles. One of them
may have given us away.

I try to run with the two
limp puckered babies
grasping my neck, still
chilly and damp, my arms
under their buttocks, their plump
legs slack. Is it too late?

Light squeezes through bamboo slats.
I squeeze my eyes shut. Corduroy
wales pleat my skin through sheets.
You're awake, humming, in the other room,
golden and rosy, blue Grow Pajamas
over scabby knees. In a minute
we will lock on the day's love, the day's rage.
In a minute I will hold you in my arms.

1977

Home, and I've

Covered the flowered linen
where I graze
on a convulvulus that hides in
lion grass, and ride in-

to the sunrise on a sand
horse. These days
shorten, but the afternoon simmered
me down. I had dinner

alone, with retrospective
on the blaz-

on of your throat's tiger-lily flush
and your salt sap enough

company until tomorrow.
The fat blue
lamp spills on a ziggurat of books,
mug the same cobalt. Looks

like reprise of lesson one
in how to
keep on keeping on. Easier, with
you fixed hours away; both

solitude and company
have a new
savor: yours. Sweet woman, I'll woman-
fully word a nomen-

clature for what we're doing
when we come
to; come to each other with our eyes,
ears, arms, minds, everything wide

open. Your tonic augments
my hum-drum
incantations till they work. I can
stop envying the man

whose berth's the lap where I'd like
to roll home
tonight. I've got May's new book for bed,
steak, greens and wine inside

me, you back tomorrow, some
words, some laz-
y time (prune the plants, hear Mozart) to
indulge in missing you.

1978

Peterborough

Another story still: a porch with trees
—maple and oak, sharpening younger shoots
against the screen; privileged solitude
with early sunlight pouring in a thin
wash on flat leaves like milk on a child's chin.
Light shifts and dulls. I want to love a woman
with my radical skin, reactionary im-
agination. My body is cored with hunger;
my mind is gnarled in oily knots of anger
that push back words: inelegant defeat
of female aspiration. First we're taught
men's love is what we cannot do without;
obliged to do without precisely that:
too fat, too smart, too loud, too shy, too old.
Unloved and underpaid, tonight untold
women will click our failings off, each bead
inflating to a bathysphere, our need
encapsulated in a metal skin,
which we, subaqueaous monsters, cannot in-
filtrate. The middle of the road is noon.
Reactive creature with inconstant moon-
tides (no doubt amendable as near-
sightedness, but sacred to How Things Are)
my blood came down and I swarmed up a tree,
intoxicated with maturity.
Woman? Well, maybe—but I was a Grown-
Up, entitled to make up my own
mind, manners, morals, myths—menses small price
to pay for midnight and my own advice.
By next September, something was revenged
on me. Muffled in sweat-soaked wool, I lunged
out of seventh-grade science lab, just quick
enough to get to the Girls' Room and be sick.
Blotched cheeks sucked to my teeth, intestines turn-
ing themselves out, hunched over a churn-
ing womb fisting itself, not quite thirteen,
my green age turned me regularly green.
Our Jewish man G.P. to whom I carried
myself hinted sex helped; once you were married.
Those weren't days I fancied getting laid.
Feet pillowed up, belly on heating pad,

head lolled toward Russian novel on the floor,
I served my time each hour of the four
days of the week of the month for the next ten
years, during which I fucked a dozen men,
not therapeutically, and just as well.
Married to boot, each month still hurt like hell.
The sky thickens, seeps rain. I retrospective-
ly add my annals to our tribe's collective
Book of Passage Rites, and do not say
a woman gave notebook leaves to me today
whose argument was what I knew: desire,
and all the old excuses ranked, conspired:
avoid, misunderstand, procrastinate;
say you're monogamous, or celibate,
sex is too messy, better to be friends
(thirsty for draughts of amity beyond
this hesitation, which has less to do
with her than my quixotic body's too
pertinacious–*tua tam pertinax*
valetudo, neither forward nor back-
ward–malingering, I ask, or healing.)
I like her: smart, strong, sane, companionate.
I still love a man: true, but irrelevant.
Then, unavaoidably, why not?
She was gone (of course) by this time; I sat
mirrored, eye-to-eye, cornered between
two scalp-high windows framing persistent rain.

1978

tua tam pertinax valetudo (Latin)–your very persistent invalidism.

Susan Griffin

I Like to Think of Harriet Tubman

I like to think of Harriet Tubman.
Harriet Tubman who carried a revolver,
who had a scar on her head from a rock thrown
by a slave-master (because she
talked back), and who
had a ransom on her head
of thousands of dollars and who
was never caught, and who
had no use for the law
when the law was wrong,
who defied the law. I like
to think of her.
I like to think of her especially
when I think of the problem of
feeding children.

The legal answer
to the problem of feeding children
is ten free lunches every month,
being equal, in the child's real life,
to eating lunch every other day.
Monday but not Tuesday.
I like to think of the President
eating lunch Monday, but not
Tuesday.
And when I think of the President
and the law, and the problem of
feeding children, I like to
think of Harriet Tubman
and her revolver.

And then sometimes
I think of the President
and other men,
men who practice the law,
who revere the law,
who make the law,
who enforce the law,
who live behind

and operate through
and feed themselves
at the expense of
starving children
because of the law.

Men who sit in paneled offices
and think about vacations
and tell women
whose care it is
to feed children
not to be hysterical
not to be hysterical as in the word
hysterikos, the greek for
womb suffering,
not to suffer in their
wombs,
not to care,
not to bother the men
because they want to think
of other things
and do not want
to take the women seriously.
I want them
to take women seriously.

I want them to think about Harriet Tubman,
and remember,
remember she was beat by a white man
and she lived
and she lived to redress her grievances,
and she lived in swamps
and wore the clothes of a man
bringing hundreds of fugitives from
slavery, and was never caught,
and led an army,
and won a battle,
and defied the laws
because the laws were wrong, I want men
to take us seriously.
I am tired wanting them to think
about right and wrong.
I want them to fear.

I want them to feel fear now
as I have felt suffering in the womb, and
I want them
to know
that there is always a time
there is always a time to make right
what is wrong,
there is always a time
for retribution
and that time
is beginning.

1971

The Song of the Woman with Her Parts Coming Out

I am bleeding
the blood seeps in red
circles on the white
white of my sheet,
my vagina
is opening, opening
closing and opening;
wet, wet,
my nipples turn rose and hard
my breasts swell against my arms
my arms float out
like anemones
my feet slide on the wooden
floor,
dancing, they are dancing, I sing,
my tongue slips from my mouth
and my mind
imagines a
clitoris
I am the woman
I am the woman
with her parts coming out
with her parts coming out.

The song of the woman with
the top of her head ripping off, with
the top of her head ripping off
and she flies out
and she flies out
and her flesh flies out
and her nose rubs against her ass,
and her eyes love ass
and her cunt
swells and sucks and waves,
and the words spring from her mind
like Fourth of July rockets,
and the words too come out,
lesbian, lesbian, lesbian, pee, pee, pee, pee, cunt, vagina,
dyke, sex, sex, sex, sex, sweat, tongue, lick, suck, sweet,
sweet, sweet, suck
and the other words march out too,
the words,
P's and Q's
the word
nice,
the word
virginity,
the word
mother,
mother goodness mother nice good goodness good good should
should be good be mother be nice good
the word
pure
the word
lascivious
the word
modest
the word
no
the word
no
the word
no
and the woman
the woman
the woman
with her

parts coming out
never stopped
never stopped
even to
say yes,
but only
flew with
her words
with her words
with her words
with her parts
with her parts
coming
with her parts
          coming
          coming
          coming
          out.

1973

This is the Story of the Day in the Life of a Woman Trying

This is the story of the day in the life of a woman trying
to be a writer and her child got sick. And in the midst of
writing this story someone called her on the telephone.
And, of course, despite her original hostile reaction to the
ring of the telephone, she got interested in the conversation
which was about teaching writing in a women's prison,
for no pay of course, and she would have done it if it
weren't for the babysitting and the lack of money for the
plane fare, and then she hung up the phone and looked
at her typewriter, and for an instant swore her original
sentence was not there. But after a while she found it. Then
she began again, but in the midst of the second sentence,
a man telephoned wanting to speak to the woman she
shares her house with, who was not available to speak on
the telephone, and by the time she got back to her type-
writer she began to worry about her sick daughter down-
stairs. And why hadn't the agency for babysitters called back
and why hadn't the department for health called back

because she was looking for a day sitter and a night sitter, one so she could teach the next day and one so she could read her poetry. And she was hoping that the people who had asked her to read poetry would pay for the babysitter since the next evening after that would be a meeting of teachers whom she wanted to meet and she could not afford two nights of babysitters let alone one, actually. This was the second day her child was sick and the second day she tried to write (she had been trying to be a writer for years) but she failed entirely the first day because of going to the market to buy Vitamin C and to the toy store to buy cutouts and crayons, and making soup from the chicken carcass that had been picked nearly clean to make sandwiches for lunch, and watering the plants, sending in the mortgage check and other checks to cover that check to the bank, and feeling tired, wishing she had a job, talking on the telephone, and putting out newspaper and glue and scissors on the kitchen table for her tired, bored child and squinting her eyes at the clock waiting for *Sesame Street* to begin again. Suddenly, after she went upstairs to her bedroom with a book, having given up writing as impossible, it was time to cook dinner. But she woke up on the second day with the day before as a lesson in her mind. Then an old friend called who had come to town whom she was eager to see and she said, "Yes, I'm home with a sick child," and they spent the morning talking. She was writing poetry and teaching she said. He had written four books he said. Her daughter showed him her red and blue and orange colored pictures. She wished he didn't have to leave so early, she thought but didn't say, and went back to pick up tissue paper off the floor and fix lunch for her and her child and begin telephoning for babysitters because she knew she had to teach the next day. And the truth was, if she did not have a sick child to care for, she was not sure she could write anyway because the kitchen was still there needing cleaning, the garden there needing weeding and watering, the living room needing curtains, the couch needing pillows, a stack of mail needing answers (for instance if she didn't call the woman who had lived in her house the month before about the phone bill soon, she would lose a lot of money). All besides, she had nothing to write. She had had fine thoughts for writing the night before but in the morning they took on a sickly complexion. And anyway, she had begun to think her life trivial and so it was, and she was tired writing the same words, or different words about the same situation, the situation or situations being that she was tired, tired of trying to write, tired of poverty or almost poverty or fear of poverty, tired of the kitchen being dirty, tired of having no lover. She was amazed that she had gotten herself dressed, actually, with thoughts like these, and caught herself saying maybe I should take a trip when she realized she had just come back from a trip and had wanted to be home so much she came back early. And even in the writing of this she thought I have written all this before and went downstairs to find her daughter had still not eaten a peanut butter sandwich and she wondered to herself what keeps that child alive?

1974

Waiting for Truth

Their bodies lined up against the walls
waiting for truth, my
words thread the room
like fishing line,
"She put
she put her head in an oven
she put her head in an
oven,"
I stutter,
my words enter space and I
slide down the line
terrified, where are we
going?
Their bodies wait for information.
"There are places I have been," I
want to tell them.
The book behind me reads:
"Sylvia Plath's range of technical resources . . ."
"There are places I have been," I
want to say, my body
all night sleeping
did I dream

running in Harlem
dream the markets of the
poor,
was someone diseased, was the disease
spreading? Did I dream
an escape? Was I safe in a
classroom, sitting close
to a friend, sighing relief,
writing the movie script,
telling where I had been,
was I singing?
Did they say my name?
That I was supposed to write words
on the chalkboard, I
was supposed to address and I
stuttered,
"What I have seen
the places I have been and I
promised everyone there
I would speak only of *them:*
the one who sat in a corner for a week,
the one whose breasts ran dry,"
And the book read,
"Sylvia Plath
Sylvia Plath's range of
technical resources was narrower
than Robert Lowell's," and I
stuttered:
"The one whose lovers
were frightened by her
children, the one who
wished her children,"
"Narrower than Robert Lowell's and so,
apparently, was her capacity"
her children would be
"for intellectual objectivity."
would be still.

The line *"Sylvia Plath's range of technical resources was narrower than Robert Lowell's and so, apparently, was her capacity for intellectual objectivity"* is from the essay "Sylvia Plath and Confessional Poetry," by M.L. Rosenthal, which appears in *The Art of Sylvia Plath*, Charles Newman, ed. (Indiana U. Press, 1971).
—*S. G.*

Sylvia Plath's range of
technical resources
she put her
was narrower
head in an
there are places I have been
Everyone on the street was diseased.
There are places you have been.
Trying to speak
the script
claiming my mind, was it
a dream
or did I live, "range of
technical."
Their bodies in transformation.
She put her head in an
repetition
repetition
is no longer
no longer
interesting in
poetry
he said
but goes on
which one put
her head in an
in life, in
autobiographical detail, gas,
milk, a pair of kids, technical resources, a bottle
of chicken fat, two dinner guests, a box of books,
Achoo IdoAchoo IdoAchoo I do
and an interesting sense of rhyme
range of
chattering, "There are places
we have," suddenly the whole
been, there are places, bodies
lined up, the walls, the whole world
suddenly the whole world is making
terrific sense I am chattering,
"Yes," I say to the bus driver, taking me home,
"I am afraid of freeways."
"Yes," I lecture a tree
near the sidewalk, "I am free."
Yes, I am afraid of rats, knives, bullets,

I am, there is, I am there is,
I sing, walking the street,
a fish on the line,
shouting to my feet,
"But I will not be afraid
of voices nor of,"
There are places we
"nor of pieces of paper."
have been.

1975

Breviary

> *I am a woman running into my own country . . . .*
> *Do not let them kill me before you speak to me,*
> *touch me, hold me.*
>
> *—Meridel le Sueur*

she is in a white dress
kneeling
K is for kneeling
in the breviary and
W is for woman,
women kneel,
small girls wear white dresses
for communion
for communion,
into the bread
the flesh,
the wine and the blood
and the women kneel
for our bread
for our blood.
Do not let them
and the woman
smiles out from her window
offering the picture-taker
a loaf of bread.
Do not let them
kill me,
stroking the soft hair

on the head
of her
baby (but we saw the second
picture, the small buttocks
in a pool of blood)
before you speak to me
and the women in white dresses
speak softly to the saints
and the saints answer,
"love befits the man
and fear befits the woman."
the words of the saints spelled
out in gold in the air
sung out by the voices
of small boys, high and light
and pure.
In the other picture one sees a woman crying,
a small old woman, holding onto a younger woman
who is also crying. And under the picture the
cameraman's words tell us that moments later
the daughter was raped and then killed.
The photographer could do nothing. The photo-
graphs were what he did. He was certain he would
be courtmartialed or killed for taking them. He
could not stop the massacres. There was nothing
he could do.
Do not let them kill me
before you speak to me
Touch me, hold me
And it might have been different if he had
been in his own country or this were not a
war because men act differently in a war.
for i am innocent.
and she removed her blouse
she showed her white neck
she opened her empty palms
she kneeled
she wept
she carried a child
she squatted down
she cried
and left a child where she had been
and she whispered to her daughter, stand

she whispered to her daughter, run
What he wanted or why he did it no one
especially knew. "She's lucky to be alive,"
the police said. She has parts of knives still
in her and knife wounds in her heart, her lung,
her liver, her spleen and her throat. She fought
him off and she lived. She is well except for
some hoarseness. The doctor does not know if her
voice will return to normal.
and the young boys voices sang out
Holy Mary
high and beautiful
Mother of God
with a red heart in her breast
and a red fruit in her mouth
and a slow movement of her thighs
the red tongue of a tiger lily
the red blood of birth
the cry of a child between her thighs
her thighs down hard
birthing the new voice
which is the end of the old voice
blood on the palms of her hands
miraculous and sudden
blood on the sheet that was white
she was in a white dress
kneeling
K is for kneeling
W is for woman
B is for bless, and bread and blood
at the hands of a man,
H is for Heathen and healing,
R is for rape, M is for massacre,
W is for woman and the words of the saints,
P is for picture and pool of blood
and for purity and prayer, for prayer and S is for she,
she,
she is in a white dress
kneeling.

1975

Fran Winant

Yesterday

(about Gertrude & Alice)

yesterday a lovely day
we traveled to the country
bouncing along in an automobile
the sun beat directly down
feeling it on my head helps me think
we bought melons at every town
until the car was filled
ate in a small restaurant
where the fish was excellent
fed the dog under the table
we returned at evening
to sit before a fire
smelling a fire-scent found in nostrils
not in air
pleasure swells from inside
to be made visible in things
that seem less than itself
in this way life is realized
through imagination

the present moment
cannot be described
without being changed
shadings of many days
make the moment that a poem is
that is why
the butter must be tasted
and the cow seen
again and again
it takes many books to equal
one taking in and letting out
of breath

a photograph caught us
walking our dog on a cobbled street
another caught us
standing in our garden

years later we are still there
new inventions
make the moment visible
but not in the same way as poetry

here
the curve of a melon
although elliptical
can be described as
an eternal circle
in which many rounds are represented
the curve of the sky, hills
and aspects of ourselves
can thus innocently be
handled and devoured
the sun that beats directly down
is like a certain light
that spreads from your fingertips
rearranging the world
as a painted canvas does
the smoothness of the tabletop
brings you close to me
although you are lying upstairs
asleep
the grain of the wood
is the line of your eyebrows

because you are always with me
it is not true
that I go off alone to write

1973

Dyke Jacket

Standing in the 14th st snack place
next to mays dept store
unable to escape my all-american reflexes
Im digging being surrounded by shitfood
watching the shopping crowd
black brown white female male kid adult

mouths all shoveling it down
some eating leathery bread envelopes
holding onions grease
bits of meat that are mostly cereal
and others eating pizza and knishes
this place has variety
Im leaning on one of those counters
where people eat standing up
with my big paper cup of black coffee
projecting myself onto
the outer edge of those taste buds
where the mozzarella cheese tomato paste
and crispy whiteflour dough
meet in a first steaming bite
Im on a diet after getting fat
trying to be a vegetarian
the way these people are
getting fat on shit
Carbohydrates did it
making me want to eat more
fatness is a form of starvation where
the more you eat the hungrier you get
and not for everyone but for me
it stands in the way of
being able to believe
I can make my body strong
there was lots of nutrition
in the nuts rice honey and seeds
but they did me in
as surely as this gleaming shit
the ultimate come-down
Im on a high protein diet meaning meat
and not eating in places like this
When I go back to vegetarianism
I promise myself I'll take a new approach
stop the shitfood joy-popping attitude
and plan meals the way its explained
in Diet For A Small Planet
which I read too late to
save myself this time
meanwhile
Im watching with the kind of fascination
that turns life into art

involvement that holds small details
making them stand for everything
as in a dream
Since last christmas
when the bathroom ceiling fell
Ive felt Ive been living past
one of the possible dates for my death
and in this place too I feel like a spirit
standing next to but outside life
having the same needs
and physical sensations
as these people
knowing intimately what a mouth is
and the slow or quick massage of eating
but having no mouth
I think perhaps this experience will
prepare me
for the spiritual side of vegetarianism
which Im beginning to see has to do with
putting a positive value on hunger
not starvation but a little unfilled hunger
all the time
its something vegetarians dont talk about

leaning on the snack bar counter
I kick the white cardboard box at my feet
to make sure its still there
inside is a snappy $8 ski-type jacket
called a flight jacket and made mostly of
reprocessed and unknown fibers
according to the tag
hanging from the zipper
Standing there with bitter coffee
in early winter daylight
Im going to take 10 minutes to gloat over
being able to get my hands on
such a desirable dyke item
Im going to wear it with satisfaction
fighting off my fears of
looking tough and ugly
enjoying my toughness
building on it not denying it
and if necessary enjoying my ugliness

affirming that too
last year I got my first pair of boys shoes
on Orchard st
this year went on my first shopping trip
to mays boys dept
who says theres no such thing as progress
had a long conversation with myself there:
maybe I dont have to buy my clothes
in *this* dept
maybe theres something just like this
in the girls dept
up the escalator to check
nothing and the closest thing is $10 more
will I look like a little boy now
or a little girl
or will I finally look like myself
in my particular combination of
the clothes I want
wonder if theres a way to look feminine
in this jacket after all
stand in front of the mirror
hands in my pockets
something about these clothes
makes me want to go along with
the wide shoulders and solid shape
I've admired the image of strength
all my life
and theres real strength not just pretense
in useful clothes
We can all be butch now and dont have to
shove that part of ourselves
which isnt only a part
off onto other women
or save it up in ourselves
for special occasions
last night I dreamed mays was having a sale
on butch roles
my sisters rushed to get theirs
average sized women like me
walked out of the store wearing
huge amazon bodies

two months ago I decided to get my hair cut
and left the Wonder Woman Beauty Salon
sporting the hairdresser Carols fantasy
of a modified 50's D.A.
"You look good with your hair back" she said
just in time for
the Bring Back the 50's Dance
where after all my protests against
glorifying our oppression
there was Marge
done up as a dyke delivery boy
complete with dark glasses in a dark room
a well-greased real D.A. haircut
straight-leg jeans a white T-shirt
cigarette behind her ear
and I realized again that
our oppression is our culture
or at least it has been
for many lesbians up to now
the role thing and the bar thing defining
the only territory where we could live out
the lies that passed for our lives
instead of the lies
that passed for someone elses
so I left the dancefloor
went into the bathroom
made my haircut into a D.A. with water
rolled up my sleeves to show my muscles
hunched my shoulders
put my hands in my pockets
went out and did the lindy
and the bunny hop
My sisters called to me, "Hi, Butch!"
and it hurt
I felt it as a condemnation
and wanted to protest no no
Im not that masculine woman
Im only playacting
the real scapegoat martyr obvious dyke
oppressor of weaker women
is somewhere else
this distrust of dykes wasnt
only in my head
it was in the way

my sisters looked at me now
the sarcastic tone of their voices
yes they meant it when they said
we should all make ourselves over
but they also meant it when they showed
they didnt know what the right kind of dyke
should look like
or how she should be treated
she couldnt be
just a certain haircut clothes mannerisms
she had to be
real skills real fighting power
but if she was actually strong
would she have to go around looking tough
and if she looked like that
should she be automatically respected
or laughed at as a phony
out to impress other women
the most tangible part of being strong is
looking strong and at that point
reality and wishful thinking get mixed
I cant dance or talk away
the negative things I associate with dykes
but at least I can live with
having my hair and clothes the way I want
my sisters encourage me
in spite of their doubts
If I can change my body
If I can become really strong
I think we'll know the difference

I walk out of the snack place
with my package swinging in one hand
and my coffee which is too hot to finish
carefully balanced in the other
I feel a happy triumph over the world
as I walk with my long stride
I feel almost comfortable
I wonder if anyone on the street
thinks I look strange

1973

Sharon Barba

Siblings

1.
He will meet me in a matched set
wanting me at last to know his lover
They speak in comparable voices
their similar histories merge
I am gaining a brother

They have paid for my ticket
and expect in return only that I be
all the dyke a boy could want
in his older sister

It will work, because I will remember
being children together,
because he told me on the phone
he always knew I was on his side

I will wear my desert boots for him
my slacks and vests, I will tell him
the history of lesbians as I know it
I will give him all the details

Next day we'll fly off again
in our Christopher-Street solidarity
bringing me, his Christmas present, home

2.
My sister will bring the baby,
the son she gave birth to as though
whenever that happened it was Christmas

Whenever she looks at me I'll
look away, remembering how he said
she refused to believe it of me,

knowing she will add them up:
two out of four, what a boon
for our side, what a loss for hers

Later I will write her a long letter
the history of tribadism as I know it

3.
All this takes place as David is
making his wedding plans
Three years she's been sneaking out
to meet him, nothing to do now but make it legal
Even her parents will bow to that, something about
the terms Husband and Wife makes people buckle under

I remember the little I know of him grown up
how he told us, looking into the mirror
he saw the world repeated over and over
inside itself smaller and smaller
until there was a world
you could sniff like a grain of coke

I could ask him how big his world is now
or what his wife will think,
marrying into a family like this one

4.
We will watch him with meaningful looks,
our baby brother, getting to be man-size
getting a man-sized cock and wanting
the girl down the street: a bad sign for our side

But we all know he reads too much,
knows too much for his years
In this family we've seen those signs before
we know where being different leads

And he may go
both ways after all,
something for everyone,
a kind of bridge
between his siblings

1972

Dykes in the Garden

One is an ex-professor of biology
the other is a stranger to us

but in their Saturday slacks
and old shirts
their hair cropped like Gertrude's

we would know them anywhere

Already we are their younger counterparts
In twenty years we will be indistinguishable

though I will go on writing my poems
and you will take my picture
under a trellis maybe

or with bare feet propped on a patio table
pencil in mouth
musing on the passions
of middle-aged Sapphics

By then we'll know how durable
the cunt is, or love itself
for that matter

working the garden together on Saturdays
stopping to talk, hands to hips
or gesturing with a spade

familiar as Gertrude and Alice
as Miss Lowell and Mrs. Russell
in their greenhouse

By then we'll know all there is to know
about dykes and gardens

strolling arm in arm, perhaps with cigars
through our own American Beauties

1974

Judith McDaniel

November Passage

1.

in early autumn darkness
I drive past the corpse a deer hung
by its antlers from the family shade tree
gutted soft white stomach slit
from crotch to throat swaying
November remembrance of summer breeze

a woman told me once:
"his oldest boy hung himself in that tree
they woke one day in August
found him there."
and as I drive
the country road in each bare tree
my mind prints a boy fifteen hanging
by his neck one hand tucked under the rope
as if to tug it away the other hand
swaying in the summer morning's breeze.

2.

we are two women
we live on this farm without men
our neighbor looks at our work
with the house and the land
too bad he warns you can't find
a man to do that for you
no locks on our doors but we own
one splitting ax three butchering knives
a sledgehammer a chainsaw and a rifle
tools of necessity.

3.

every day in autumn
our cat presents a corpse as the mice
come into the house for winter
when she doesn't return for days
I search and find her lying in the mud

healing the wounds in her side
I see muscle and bone and grey
tissue   around each hole
and I wonder if she stalked this fox
or wandered into violence unaware.

4.

last spring I got two dozen chicks
let them peck and grow   but now in autumn
I must choose to build a house
and feed them   or kill them
I read a book   go down to the yard
with my ax and knife   I read a book
and boil the water   take the bird
in one hand   the book said
ax in the other   lay the bird's head
on the chopping block   wild unmanageable
now insane   flapping   cackling   clawing
one hen's wings beat my face   rake my arms
her reluctance to die   heats me
in a fury   I kill four
and carry them in my scratched arms
to the bucket of boiling water   dip
hang and pluck   slit the still warm
flesh   knife tearing cardboard   and I
pull out the yellow and green intestines
the swollen golden gizzard   I kill twenty
birds   then give the rest to friends
the smell of blood and wet feathers
grown too strong   and all this winter
I will eat chicken stew made from birds I killed
and smell wet feather and see the ax
and the plucked yellowpink bodies hanging
from my clothesline

5.

our neighbor   brings us venison
to be served with turkey for Thanksgiving
two red-faced boys stand behind him
in my kitchen   their eyes slide
from me   to dill weed feathering

down a rafter   I cannot eat
the meat   nor refuse their gift.
I wonder   who killed the deer
and who will kill the bird.

6.

swaying in the summer breeze
a piece of rope   two bales of hay to stand on
and kick away   one hand tucked under the rope
beside his neck tugging at the tightness
across his throat   white and soft
and his neck broken   the book said
place the head   on the chopping block
the ax in his father's hand   knuckles scraped
an irish drunk and a scotchman's fury
and he swung   in that tree.

1978

Julie Blackwomon

Revolutionary Blues

and when I say to my sisters
my lesbian feminist sisters
my angry white sisters whose chains still mesh with mine
when I say sisters help me
the noose tightens on my neck
I cannot breathe
                    it is because I am black
my sisters say
                yes,
but what has that to do
                        with our revolution?
and when I say to my brothers
my angry black brothers with leopard dashikis
whose roots entwine with mine in Africa
when I say brothers help me
I am encircled by fire
the flames grow nearer
                it is because I love women
my brothers say
                    yes,
but what has that to do with our revolution?

and when the revolution comes
and it is time for choosing sides
when radical lesbian feminists
are fighting our oppression by men

and when the revolution comes
and it is time for choosing sides
when militant black nationalists
are fighting our oppression by whites
I expect to be shot in the back
by someone who calls me sister.

1976

Martha Shelley

The Tree of Begats

When they offered me the glass
I turned it down.

The baby sucked a rubber nipple
dipped in wine, and fell asleep again.
Ruddy little nephew,
covered with the fuzz of monkey ancestors,
thrust from a tropical womb
into a blue flannel blanket.
The rabbi tried to bring my godson
closer to the angels,
cutting off that other vestige of an ape,
the little sheath of skin around his cock.

These clean-shaven rabbis merely pretend to reform,
saying, in English, "Thank God for a healthy child"
and in the ancient tongue
" . . . for giving us a son as our first-born."

The women, in vernacular,
clustered around a tray of cocktail franks,
glancing sideways at my track shoes
visible beneath a velvet pants suit.
The glass came round.
"All those who want sons, drink,"
the rabbi said. They sipped a bit.
I turned it down.

"Hey, ma," I said, "I have a radio show."
"Cousin Lynne, I wrote these poems."
"Dad, hey listen, dad,
I got a yellow belt in my karate class."
"Hey, ma . . .?"

The women cornered me around the canapes.
"It's your turn now."
"When are you going to make your mother
twice a grandma?"

No way. My womb, like my fist,
is clenched against the world.

Kid sister, I remember being three,
climbing the bars of your crib
teaching you to clap
and sing some garbled Yiddish rhyme.
You asked the wishing well
for a red pinafore.
I, for a microscope.

We rattle around in different cages now.
You almost became your mother's daughter.
I am each day less the wandering lesbian
my father dares not own.

Our eyes meet over a barricade
of sanctified penises
and I ask myself why sisterhood
sometimes feels like a wine glass
crushed in my fist.

1974

Bobbie Bishop

grandmother's little feet
carried seven children
cataracts
into 90 years
piscean
piscean
1884 brought
her blue eyes in
and a long time
to endure
churches
wagons
five daughters
two sons
a salty veterinary
journalist farmer
patriarch until
death he at
87 did part.
my grandmother
tell me, a lesbian
granddaughter who is
spread so differently
on life's bread . . .
respectfully
who are you
at a sixty year distance
grandmother Myrtle
'any of several
evergreen shrubs'
you of small stature
fuzzy permanent hair
brown still at 65
your voice
communicating always
a special pain
a common singing
to a granddaughter
who carries your genes on
picking new messages
mutating deliberately
into a woman's wool.

c. 1975

Rita Mae Brown

Sappho's Reply

My voice rings down through thousands of years
To coil around your body and give you strength,
You who have wept in direct sunlight,
Who have hungered in invisible chains,
Tremble to the cadence of my legacy:
An army of lovers shall not fail.

1969

Pat Parker

This at last is bone of my bones
and flesh of my flesh;
she shall be called Woman,
because she was taken out of
Man.

Genesis I:23

from cavities of bones
spun
from caverns of air
i, woman–bred of man
taken from the womb of sleep;
i, woman that comes
before the first.

to think second
to believe first
a mistake
erased by the motion of years.
i, woman, i
can no longer claim
a mother of flesh
a father of marrow
I, Woman must be
the child of myself.

1968

A Small Contradiction

It is politically incorrect
to demand monogamous
relationships–

It's emotionally insecure
to seek
ownership of

another's soul—
or body &
damaging to one's psyche
to restrict the giving and
taking of love.

Me, i am
totally opposed to
monogamous relationships
unless
i'm
in love.

1972

For Willyce

When i make love to you
i try
with each stroke of my tongue
to say i love you
to tease i love you
to hammer i love you
to melt i love you

& your sounds drift down
oh god!
oh jesus!
and i think—
here it is, some dude's
getting credit for what
a woman
has done,
again.

1972

Movement in Black
movement in Black
can't keep em back
movement in Black

1.
They came in ships
from a distant land
bought in chains
to serve the man

I am the slave
that chose to die
I jumped overboard
& no one cried

I am the slave
sold as stock
walked to and fro
on the auction block

They can be taught
if you show them how
they're strong as bulls
and smarter than cows.

I worked in the kitchen
cooked ham and grits
seasoned all dishes
with a teaspoon of spit.

I worked in the fields
picked plenty of cotton
prayed every night
for the crop to be rotten.

All slaves weren't treacherous
that's a fact that's true
but those who were
were more than a few.

Movement in Black
Movement in Black
Can't keep em back
Movement in Black

2.
I am the Black woman
& i have been all over
when the colonists
fought the British
i was there
i aided the colonist
i aided the British
i carried notes,
stole secrets,
guided the men
& nobody thought
to bother me
i was just a
Black woman
the britishers lost
and I lost,
but I was there
& i kept on moving

I am the Black woman
& i have been all over
i went out west, yeah
the Black soldiers
had women too,
& i settled the land,
& raised crops & children,
but that wasn't all
i hauled freight,
& carried mail,
drank plenty whiskey
shot a few men too.
books don't say much
about what I did
but I was there
& i kept on moving.

I am the Black woman
& i have been all over
up on platforms & stages
talking about freedom
freedom for Black folks
freedom for women
In the civil war too
carrying messages,
bandaging bodies
spying and lying
the south lost
& i still lost
but i was there
& i kept on moving

I am the Black woman
& I have been all over
I was on the bus
with Rosa Parks
& in the streets
with Martin King
I was marching
and singing
and crying
and praying
I was with SNCC
& i was with CORE
I was in Watts
when the streets
were burning
I was a panther
in Oakland
In New York
with N.O.W.
In San Francisco
with gay liberation
in D.C. with
the radical dykes
yes, I was there
& i'm still moving

movement in Black
movement in Black

can't keep em back
movement in Black

3.
I am the Black woman

I am Bessie Smith
singing the blues
& all the Bessies
that never sang a note

I'm the southerner
who went north
I'm the northerner
who went down home

I'm the teacher
in the all Black school
I'm the graduate
who cannot read

I'm the social worker
in the city ghetto
I'm the car hop
in a delta town

I'm the junkie with a jones
I'm the dyke in the bar
I'm the matron at county jail
I'm the defendant with nothin' to say.

I'm the woman with 8 kids
I'm the woman who didn't have any
I'm the woman who poor as sin
I'm the woman who's got plenty.

I'm the woman who
raised white babies &
taught my kids to
raise themselves.

movement in Black
movement in Black
can't keep em back
movement in Black

4.
Roll call, shout em out

Phyliss Wheatley
Sojourner Truth
Harriet Tubman
Frances Ellen Watkins Harper
Stagecoach Mary
Lucy Prince
Mary Pleasant
Mary McLeod Bethune
Rosa Parks
Coretta King
Fannie Lou Hamer
Marian Anderson
& Billies
& Bessie
sweet Dinah
A-re-tha
Natalie
Shirley Chisholm
Barbara Jordan
Patricia Harris
Angela Davis
Flo Kennedy
Zora Neale Hurston
Nikki Giovanni
June Jordan
Audre Lorde
Edmonia Lewis
and me
and me
and me
and me
and me
& all the names we forgot to say
& all the names we didn't know
& all the names we don't know, yet.

movement in Black
movement in Black
Can't keep em back
movement in Black

5.
I am the Black woman
I am the child of the sun
the daughter of dark
I carry fire to burn the world
I am water to quench its throat
I am the product of slaves
I am the offspring of queens
I am still as silence
I flow as the stream

I am the Black woman
I am a survivor
I am a survivor
I am a survivor
I am a survivor
I am a survivor

Movement in Black.

1977

This poem was first performed at Oakland Auditorium on December 2nd and 3rd 1977 by Linda Tillery, Vicki Randle, Alberta Jackson, Mary Watkins, and Pat Parker.

—P.P.

Where Will You Be?

Boots are being polished
Trumpeters clean their horns
Chains and locks forged
The crusade has begun.

Once again flags of Christ
are unfurled in the dawn

and cries of soul saviors
sing apocalyptic on air waves.

Citizens, good citizens all
parade into voting booths
and in self-righteous sanctity
X away our right to life.

I do not believe as some
that the vote is an end,
I fear even more
It is just a beginning.

So I must make assessment
Look to you and ask:
Where will you be
when they come?

They will not come
a mob rolling
through the streets,
but quickly and quietly
move into our homes
and remove the evil,
the queerness,
the faggotry,
the perverseness
from their midst.
They will not come
clothed in brown,
and swastikas, or
bearing chest heavy with
gleaming crosses.
The time and need
for ruses are over.
They will come
in business suits
to buy your homes
and bring bodies to
fill your jobs.
They will come in robes
to rehabilitate
and white coats

to subjugate
and where will you be
when they come?

Where will we *all be*
when they come?
And they will come–

they will come
because we are
defined as opposite–
perverse
and we are perverse.

Every time we watched
a queer hassled in the
streets and said nothing–
It was an act of perversion.

Everytime we lied about
the boyfriend or girlfriend
at coffee break–
It was an act of perversion.

Everytime we heard,
"I don't mind gays
but why must they
be blatant?" and said nothing–
It was an act of perversion.

Everytime we let a lesbian mother
lose her child and did not fill
the courtrooms–
It was an act of perversion.

Everytime we let straights
make out in our bars while
we couldn't touch because
of laws–
It was an act of perversion.

Everytime we put on the proper
clothes to go to a family

wedding and left our lovers
at home—
It was an act of perversion.

Everytime we heard
"Who I go to bed with
is my personal choice—
It's personal not political"
and said nothing—
It was an act of perversion.

Everytime we let straight relatives
bury our dead and push our
lovers away—
It was an act of perversion.

And they will come.
They will come for
the perverts

& it won't matter
if you're
    homosexual, not a faggot
    lesbian, not a dyke
    gay, not queer
It won't matter
if you
    own your business
    have a good job
    or are on S.S.I.
It won't matter
if you're
    Black
    Chicano
    Native American
    Asian
    or White
It won't matter
if you're from
    New York
    or Los Angeles
    Galveston
    or Sioux Falls

It won't matter
if you're
    Butch, or Fem
    Not into roles
    Monogamous
    Non Monogamous
It won't matter
If you're
    Catholic
    Baptist
    Atheist
    Jewish
    or M.C.C.

They will come
They will come
to the cities
and to the land
to your front rooms
and in *your* closets.

They will come for
the perverts
and where will
you be
When they come?

1978

M. C. C.—Metropolitan Community Church, a lesbian and gay male church.

Melanie Kaye

Brooklyn 1956: The Walls Are Full of Noise

Only the bathroom
is private. I lock myself in
for peace, lock out
my daddy's voice:
"Is that kid still in there?"
I don't care.
I claim constipation.
I sit on the pot and read
baseball novels. I am
the Dodgers' first woman pitcher,
my dream breasts poke through my sweater.
Karl Spooner loves me.
Everyone strikes out.

Or else I read black stallion novels.
Someone gives me a horse with white feet
(called socks). We gallop
down Flatbush Avenue
where Spauldings pop on the trolley tracks.
Together we snatch Naomi whose hair curls in ringlets
out of the streetcar's rollicking path.

I dream of having my own room,
a bed with a bedspread,
a velvet canopy, red with gold tassels.
There are shelves for tiny glass rabbits,
porcelain turtles, everything small
for the pocket. This room is modeled
on Ellen Kay's, she moved to a Long Island kitchen
with tile linoleum, an upstairs,
two
bathrooms.
"Turn off the water," she told me,
"We pay for it."
Pay for water?
I thought she was making it up
to be mean.

We are 6-D and water comes last to us,
showers are risky, I pop out red and soapy
when anyone turns on cold. If I howl
they hear it in 5-D where Mrs. Hirsch
uses our water up. Mrs. Hirsch
is divorced, dyes her hair black.
She and her daughter Paulette shriek
I HATE YOU at 2 in the morning.

Above us the roof where I tiptoe
through flapping sheets which smack my face
to spread an old towel on the hot tar.
I dream of leaping from roof to roof
till I scramble down red brick and glass
onto a balcony with sliding windows
where rich people feed me cookies and juice.

Across the alley a neighbor shouts
"Get off the roof" at least twice a week
to the peeping tom who hangs out up there
to watch us dress.
Once the cops came and looked bored.
We give up pulling the shades,
we get used to his secret eyes.
"Hey Tom, nice of you
to see us again,"
we shout back
across the deep alley.

1977

Trojan

for the women of Bella Cosa who occupied Trojan Nuclear Power Plant, November 1977

driving
a wooded stretch
beside the quick Columbia
where fish are dying—
then we see
a tower jabbing the sky

we crouched for the 5-bell drill
hands over eyes, squirming
to keep skirts down

closer
one side of the tower is wet. you say,
moss will grow there.
you say, *barnacles form on the waste pipes*
unlike any barnacles seen before.
you say, *they train ferrets to run through the tubings*
dragging a dustcloth. you say,
they call them maids.

for the first 6 months
we give milk 6 times a day
part food, part poison

crouched by the gate
we talk of men who sign papers
to put poison into the air.
they wear hats of skin
and coats stitched by women,
cleaned and brushed by women.
they eat meals prepared by women,
part food, part poison

tilted in chairs on the upper floors
of various downtown office buildings
mopped at night by women
do they dream
how moss whispers up the side?

in the makeshift jail
we tug our wrists free from plastic handcuffs.
when they take my coat, you give your sweater

under their noses
our hands
are easy to hide

1978

Honor Moore

First Time: 1950

In the back bedroom, laughing when you pull
something fawn-colored from your black
tight pants, the unzipped chino slit.
I keep myself looking at the big belt
buckled right at my eyes, feel the hand
riffle my hair: You are called Mouse, baby-

sitter trusted Wednesdays with my baby
brother. With me. I still see you pull
that huge bunch of keys from a pocket, hand
them to my brother, hear squeaking out back
Mrs. Fitz's clothesline as you unbelt,
turn me to you, my face to the open slit.

It's your skin, this thing, head, its tiny slit
like the closed eye of a still-forming baby:
As you stroke, it stiffens like a new belt—
your face gets almost sick. I want to pull
away, but you grip my arm: I tell by your black
eyes you won't let go. With your left hand

you take my chin. With your other hand
you guide it, head reddening, into my slit,
my five-year old mouth. In the tight black
quiet of my shut eyes, I hear my baby
brother shaking the keys. You lurch, pull
at my hair. I don't breathe, feel buckle, belt,

pant. It tastes lemony, musty as a belt
after a day of sweat. Mouth hurts, my hands
push, push at your hips. I gag. You let me pull
free. I open my eyes, see the strange slits
yours are; you don't look at me. "Babe, babee—"
You are moaning, almost crying. The black

makes your skin clam-white now, your jewel-black
eyes blacker. You buckle up the thick belt.
When you take back the keys, my baby

brother cries. You extend a shaking hand
you make kind. In daylight through the wide slit
an open shade leaves, I see her pull,

Mrs. Fitz pulling in her rusty, soot-black
line. Framed by the slit, her window, her large hands
flash, sort belts, dresses, shirts, baby clothes.

1978

Poem: For the Beginning

Noon, the sky gray, the snow not falling in earnest, so
the day seems odd, too usual, almost boring, the light
        from the slight new cover on the old snow not
broken, played by the sun with color, but flat, intensely
                white. This morning a woman was saying,
                        separation is good for
        love. She has been here a month, I two days, and
this new snow on old ice is slippery: I have fallen
twice. Weeks ago, I said, I want to be only happy
        with you, and you said, there are always other
feelings. What I mean is, I want to care for you, care as
                for the most delicate plant or creature, care
                        as one guards a singular
        gift which is fragile, beautiful. Last night, on
the telephone, we tried to arrange your visit. You
couldn't say, definitely yes, because a nearly past
        love will visit, and you must see her, so you
cannot tell me yes, definitely, this day, because
                she has not said definitely, yes, that
                        day. Last night on a pay phone,
        we talked an hour, bare bulb dangling, giving
light, I tracing my returned dime with purple ball point,
moving the dime, drawing in its circle first a face,
        then hair. I say, I don't trust what happens when
you are with her, scribble out eyes, mouth, move the dime, trace
                another. I'm feeling what might be my
                        love for you like a change in
        temperature, wondering if I must be unsure
to feel it. This circle stays hollow. I scratch out from
its edge, flames, as if the sun were purple, eclipsed by a white

dime moon. I wish she'd disappear, I say, and
regret it. Let's not talk about her, you say, your hair
flooding my mind like coal-colored water,
black, rushing from thick ice
on the river in town, black tongue flooding out
from white lips, endless, thawing. I want to be only
happy with you, not held back. I want to care for you as
for a delicate plant. I want you to care
for me. A woman near the fire says, I have found love
this way between women: a see-saw, one up,
the other . . . Care for you as
I want to hold you, my legs firm, your body
resisting their force, care as I want my mouth moving
against yours, as it does, as it has against no one else's
mouth, care as I want to lie beside you, our
faces close, dark, and look into you through your cordovan
eyes. *Separation is good for . . . This way . . .*
a see-saw . . . Jealousy and
possession, the woman says, are our least
legitimized feelings. *You to care for me.* This
day, light stays the same, trees don't move—silence, then an
occasional creak, the oil burner
roaring, measuring time by cold and heat—on, off, on . . .
The six-pronged shell, gift from you, balances
on its transparent stand, seems
to float, image of heat, pink center of heat
burning out, still and continuing, as if the hot
color of a daylily opening were heat rather
than color. This cold between us is distance,
circumstance. Just how, I ask her, is separation good?
Going away, she says, coming back—almost
waving her hand as she speaks,
I like coming back, leaving and coming back. Coming back.

1978

Elise Young

1.
The First Separation

must have been a relief—of our
own volitition after all it was time
time to issue from the womb time to
enter time with or without you making it
at breakneck speed neck and back bent backwards
feet in the air a trial by light a trial to
breathe and be
heard

but it was hard the heads came last
you see it must have been a terrible hurry
for both of us; for us both trouble
trouble to breathe and be heard the long wrack
of night at our backs the cruel cool quiet
of the womb left behind for the cool cruel
wrack of the night

and the scythe, the cool steel of the forceps
that bit my arm, broke it in two

2.
Then there was a difference.
But let me say this carefully.
Then there was a difference
between us.
Arm distended or swollen a tooth that
popped sooner or later.
Time the filter time the lead time
the warden, kept us different and the same.
We grew to a balloon lopsided and funny
we grew in this way—always being
measured

3.
In the picture the Siamese twins who worked
out their separation/one slept while
the other played

are holding hands, the operation is successful
and she reaches over to touch an
other

what is in her touch

Can anyone imagine how this feels and you
and I who spoke of this over and over
imagining the scars, living with the
fear and longing.
The welding process was so careful so complete
and so subtle how could I have known or you
that you were not different from me
but different/an other/a difference

what is in her touch
Did I reach over in my sleep to choke you or
to heal you

Were my nightmares my only escape into solitude?

She wrote and said: we both have breasts and
vaginas blood flows every month and it is the same.
I keep meaning to tell you—I love you, in a world
where separation is pain where separation is oblivion

Though we wore the same costume and now must
rename
Though violence has held us together like rats in a
maze though coupled till separation was suffocation
and suffocation was being the same
Though I have had to make myself indifferent and to blame
seizing hold of your tears till they flowed well
though to fight to love in this land where
every woman is different and the same
woman sister sharer of the womb some kind of lover
I love your blood and your cramps that are vanished
I love your shame and your courage your self-
protection your bullying your laughter your name
and if you can say it—your willingness not to die for me
but to survive

1972

Willyce Kim

The men of some Native American Tribes had shields which hung outside of their lodgings. The shields depicted the movements of their lives—past, present, and future dreams. The women of the tribes rarely made shields; they wore belts which were the equivalent of the shields.

Month of May: Moon when the ponies shed

A Woman's Tribal Belt

In the Moon
when the ponies had shed
when the flowers of summer
tore down the stones of winter
and turned them under my feet;
when the knuckles
of my clenched fist
rose like five white suns
into a cloudless sky.

In the Moon
of the shedding ponies
the winds from the north
dive down
dive under
from the hot breath
of my sisters.
Shoulders are locked
against shoulders.

In the Moon
when the ponies will shed
when the pale of my skin
matches the colors
of the crushed earth
I will raise up my ear
against your breast
and listen for the nation
that lives within you.

1973

Keeping Still, Mountain

for Kit-fan

You bring me silver and turquoise
from the mountains,
and red onions from your garden.
I give you miso soup,
and wear your coat from China.
Tea steeps in porcelain cups.
Night sounds fill the air.

1980

Ana Kowalkowska

Azteca IV

En mis sueños quiero enseñar quiero abogar quiero gritar quiero matar	In my dreams I want to teach I want to advocate I want to scream I want to kill
En mis sueños quiero captar los momentos pocos bonitos que hay en ésta	In my dreams I want to capture the few beautiful moments that are in this
En mis sueños quiero ser la presidenta quiero ser la mecánica	In my dreams I want to be the president I want to be the mechanic
En mis sueños no veo hombres que ahora 'ay veo mujeres y veo la gente	In my dreams I do not see men that now are I see the women I see the people
En mis sueños quiero se la fotografa quiero ser la poeta azteca	In my dreams I want to be the photographer I want to be the aztec poet
En mis sueños veo el arco iris de la Raza sol borrando el de blanco	In my dreams I see the rainbow of La Raza sun obliterating white
En mis sueños quiero comer quiero dormir	In my dreams I want to eat I want to sleep

quiero correr
quiero andar

En mis sueños
aborezco
a los pinches
cabrones viejos
que nos pisan

En mis sueños
quiero amar
quiero luchar
quiero tener
quiero darles
quiero querer

En mis sueños
quiero educar
a los pinches
respiro, y los
asesino

En mis sueños
diarios lloro
río digo
y vivo esta
pesadilla

En mis sueños
diarios callo
grito, juego
trabajo es
vivir dicen

En mis sueños
no te enojes
dicen eres
chicana eres
mujer, no eres

I want to run
I want to walk

In my dreams
I hate
the charlie fuckers
the charlie fuckers
that stomp us

In my dreams
I want to love
I want to fight
I want to have
I want to give to you
I want to want

In my dreams
I want to educate
the fuckers
I breathe y I
assassinate them

In my dreams
daily I cry
I laugh I tell
I live this
nightmare

In my dreams
daily I am quiet
I scream, I play
I work it is
to live they say

In my dreams
don't be angry
they say you are
chicana, you are
woman, you are not

En mis sueños
las velitas
de mi alma
prenden con
esperanzas

Tu hermana
Tu me prendes
Tu hermano
    no me
        apagarás
            verás

In my dreams
the tapers
of my soul
light with
hopes

You sister
you light me
you brother
    you don't put
        me out
            you see

1974

Spanish original and English translation by Ana Kowalkowska.

Minnie Bruce Pratt

Oconeechee Mountain

My mother always said
make the most of what you've got.

So the year I lived in the country
I had as friends only
those aloof and undemanding acquaintances
true and false solomon's seal
purple toadflax
the red-shouldered hawk.

I conjugated only with Ovid and my husband,
manipulated my breasts to toughen them for babies,
and flank jammed against
that of the hill above the Eno,
masturbated as unselfconsciously as Eve,

watching the ferns uncurl above my face,
the sun govern in slow degrees
the unfolding of elm and trillium.

1976

Rape

At four in the morning I hear
        her scream again.
This time he holds the knife
        to her throat in the park
behind my house where leaves
        darken for the fall.
She offers thirty-two cents.
        He wants all.
When the police come they don't
        find no screaming
lady search the creepers
        at next light
find no body left

but the corpse
of my fear clutching the phone
on the desk and wait

for her to scream again
at ten in the morning
down by the creek it's Sue
taken fishing by her grand-
father, raped and hooked
by him with pain

in the fall, in the early
afternoon
watching the bees bloom
in the sasanquas
I hear my lover scream
in Kansas City
where he holds the knife close
to her white throat
where she fights while blood drips
from her ears to the floor

behind a barracks door
slammed in Germany
Sue hesitates to scream,
to create a stir,
a racist scene over the black
GI beating
off his load of rage
in her

final report of the day
I hear Beth
typing the women who've sat
in her office, their lives
bleeding from the mouth, their sides
swollen with incest,
they slide into the metal
file drawers
while Beth feels them murmur and cry
in the cabinet of her heart

Mesia measures the red
  for Holofernes'
head and paints revenge
  for her rape and death,
paints Judith alive with the knife
  in the shadows of midnight

I wake to my lover's scream
  this time in my arms
he holds the knife to her throat.
  Her scars bleed.
I think of Holofernes'
  bleeding head,
I hold a knife to his throat.
  I hold her.
We watch the dark night pass.
  The door is locked.
We hear the step. He holds
  the knife to her throat.
I hold her, scarred. I hold
  her in my arms.

1977

The Sound of One Fork

Through the window screen I can see an angle of grey roof
and the silence that spreads in the branches of the pecan tree
as the sun goes down. I am waiting for a lover. I am alone
in a solitude that vibrates like the cicada in hot midmorning,
that waits like the lobed sassafras leaf just before
its dark green turns into red, that waits
like the honey bee in the mouth of the purple lobelia.

While I wait, I can hear the random clink of one fork
against a plate. The woman next door is eating supper
alone. She is sixty, perhaps, and for many years
has eaten by herself the tomatoes, the corn
and okra that she grows in her backyard garden.
Her small metallic sound persists, as quiet almost
as the windless silence, persists like the steady

random click of a redbird cracking a few
more seeds before the sun gets too low.
She does not hurry, she does not linger.

Her younger neighbors think that she is lonely,
that only death keeps her company at meals.
But I know what sufficiency she may possess.
I know what can be gathered from year to year,
gathered from what is near to hand, as I do
elderberries that bend in damp thickets by the road,
gathered and preserved, jars and jars shining
in rows of claret red, made at times with help,
a friend or a lover, but consumed long after,
long after they are gone and I sit
alone at the kitchen table.

And when I sit in the last heat of Sunday
afternoons on the porch steps in the acid breath of the boxwoods,
I also know desolation and consider death as an end.
The week is over, the night that comes will not lift.
I am exhausted from making each day.
My family and children are in other states,
the women I love in other towns. I would rather be here
than with them in the old ways, but when all that's left
of the sunset is the red reflection underneath the clouds,
when I get up and come in to fix supper
in the darkened kitchen I am often lonely for them.

In the morning and the evening we are by ourselves,
the woman next door and I. Sometimes we are afraid
of the death in solitude and want someone
else to live our lives. Still we persist.
I open the drawer to get out the silverware.
She goes to her garden to pull weeds and pick
the crookneck squash that turns yellow with late summer.
I walk down to the pond in the morning to watch
and wait for the blue heron who comes at first light
to feed on minnows that swim through her shadow in the water.
She stays until the day grows so bright
that she cannot endure it and leaves with her hunger unsatisfied.
She bows her wings and slowly lifts into flight,
grey and slate blue against a paler sky.
I know she will come back. I see the light create

a russet curve of land on the farther bank
where the wild rice bends heavy and ripe
under the first blackbirds. I know
she will come back. I see the light curve
in the fall and rise of her wing.

1979

My mother loves women.
She sent me gold and silver
earrings for Valentine's Day.
She sent a dozen red roses
to Ruby Lemley when she
was sick and took her 8 quarts
of purplehull peas, shelled
and ready to cook.
She walks every evening
down our hill and around
with Margaret Hallman.
They pick up loose hub caps
and talk about cataracts
and hysterectomies.
At the slippery spots
they go arm in arm.

She has three sisters,
Evie, Ora Gilder, and Lethean.
Sometimes when they aggravate her,
she wants to pinch their habits off them,
like potatobugs off the leaf.
But she still meets them each weekend
for cards and jokes while months go by
without her speaking to her brother
who plays dominoes at the bus stop with the men.
She doesn't seem to have known
a man except this brother Robert
and my father who for the last 20 years
has been waiting for death in his rocking
chair in front of the TV set.

During that time my mother
was seeing women every day
at work in her office. She knit them

intricate afghans and told me proudly
that Anne Ogletree could not
go to sleep without hers.

My mother loves women but
she's afraid to ask me
about my life.
She thinks that I might
love women too.

1979

The Segregated Heart

First Home

Nowadays I call no one place home.

For awhile it was a house on the highest land around,
a hill that lightning always struck during the summer
storms when I watched the sky go green and black
and suddenly begin to move. Then the trees belonged
less to the ground than to the upper air.
The oaks and hickories bent almost to break,
their leaves turned inside out by gusts of rain,
their branches whirling, vanished, reappeared
quick as the fire that leapt up in the distance
to shatter itself in branching veins of light,
then instantly be whole again. From within, I heard
the thunder, the clouds travel to the edge of the hills.
I wanted to take their motion for my own and yet
I wanted to stay to see the new leaves reflecting
in the sun millions of green mirrors hanging from the trees.

Within the house down the narrow hallway
in the small rooms we lived each day the same:
politely and in silence we ate in the kitchen,
I took my napkin from the silver ring that bore my name,
my mother helped us to food while Laura who had cooked it

"the segregated heart"— Lillian Smith.

went to sit in a chair in another room. My father
always thanked her as we left the table.

Laura and I sat long afternoons without talking.
I could not understand her words, like harsh foreign language.
But the afternoon I found her in the front room,
sprawled and drunk on the flowered rug, I heard her breath
rattle through the house to join the others,
the sudden noises made by those partitioned into sorrow,
the weeping of my mother late at night behind a door,
the rush of water she used to drown her bitter sound,
the weeping of my father, drunk at dawn by the window
when he saw the green edge of light on the top of the oak,
the click of his chair as he rocked and cursed himself,
the sounds made by those who believed they had to stay
while their hearts broke in every room of the house.

Each noon we returned to our places in the kitchen.
For us change came from the outside and brought no good
like the thunderstorms that swept down north from Birmingham
or the elm blight that cleared town square of trees and left
the stone soldier standing guard alone over my father's fathers,
names written in marble honor on his weathered base.

There we used habit to contain, to outlast despair.
Even in the cemetery where my father's mother,
where my namesake lay, barbed wire ran between the graves,
dividing white folk from the black, it ran between
the women setting lilies on one side, the women hoeing on the other,
a fence to separate one heap of bare red clay from another.

Second Home

I have lived in rented houses, where I learned
to stare at walls at 4 a.m. with a sick child
sprawled across my lap, a husband asleep in another room,
where I considered the interior decoration of walls:
which pictures I would hang in the blank spaces
if I could choose. I began to understand the manners
of walls: to pretend I didn't see that they were there.
I began to refuse, would not sew or hang the curtains,
left the windows bare, unveiled and watched the light
spread over the sills out to its limit on the floor.

I studied the history of walls: the white and yellow sandstone,
the blue glaze around women held in a persian harem,
the windowless brick of a factory where I once sewed
with a hundred other women, black and white
(but men only were allowed to cut the cloth).
I studied the sociology of walls: the rotten boards
crumbling like bark on a fallen log, dropping
from the outside of Laura's house in the quarter,
the chainlink fence seen by women from where they stood
ironing their uniforms in the prison laundry,
on the 500 block the cracked plaster ceiling stared at
by a woman in a bed in a cubicle rented by a pimp.

I learned the anger of walls: they had kept me from myself.
Before I left, the live oak in the front yard fell on the porch.
I saw with satisfaction the crushed bricks and mortar:
his house was not mine. I kissed another woman,
not for manners but for love, and felt all shift around me,
as if I stood outside on a clay bank after a heavy rain,
as if the ground slid under my feet to settle in another place.

But I was surprised when my mother called to tell me
a tornado had come like a hundred freight trains,
rolled over her hill, lifted the roof from the house.
She said the trees were gone: the water oaks, the blackjack oaks,
the sweetgum and poplar, the magnolia grandiflora.
I had wanted motion and all was changed. With anger and love
I had changed and now I had no home. I was left
in a place I had never been, where the slope lay open and dry,
spiked with purple nettle and wild lettuce, the few trees left
standing dead, bark scaling from their sides,
like woods I'd seen stripcut for the saw mill.
My family were strangers from another country. They spoke
from a long way away and in a different language.

I learned the grief of walls: to leave where I could not stay,
to bend myself to change was to leave where I also loved.
Later my mother wrote that the kudzu was taking the hill
(after rain the vine spread, green veins held together the red dirt).
She wrote that the storm had set out canna lilies
(they flourished, broke open into red fragile lobes of bloom).

Third Home

The radio says flooding in Mississippi and parts of Alabama.
Outside my door the rain washes pollen in a yellow stream
off the porch and down the steps. The pines have been in bloom
for the last week, the wind moves through them in gusts
and becomes visible in sudden yellow clouds that lift from the trees.
Inside my house, my floors, my clothes are thick with yellow dust.

Before the storm broke, I watched the bees investigate
the corners of my porch, the oval bell of my wind chimes,
looking for a home before their swarm. I know inside the hive
the virgin workers lie, with bent head and folded arm,
each sealed within her quiet cell until waked from larval sleep
by the dance and beating wings of her sisters. At first flight
each fears to leave behind the fixed prismatic form,
each soars and returns twenty times, hesitates at the void of space,
the indistinct brilliant mass of colors, the yellow and blue,
the wind that twists her to and from her course.
She shrinks at first from the infinite loneliness of light
but knows she can return to the translucent walls of honeycomb
where her sisters work and others wait to be born.

I live with no sister and have no daughter to name or raise.
I have no home except what I make for myself. Today it is
three rooms surrounded by rain where thunder cracks,
rolls through open windows, continues through the distances.
What I left I will not return to; yet I live in it every day.
The radio says mill workers in Wilson have brown lungs,
their cells of pink flesh filled up with cotton dust.
The radio reports four women in Memphis, on foot from a dance,
shotgunned: they bled through small pellet wounds,
bright red holes in their dark skin and evening clothes.
The police see no connection between this and two crosses
burned in town that night, white flames fixed at right angles.

If I stand in the doorway, the storm drowns out the radio.
I put my hands in the rain, louder than rushing blood,
colder than the tears of my anger or despair. My home is not safe
but dangerous with pain that aches like a cracked bone healing.
I refuse the divisions; yet always they break again.
I miss my mother and Laura who raised me; they still live
in the same and in different houses. I live here knowing

that the separation ends only when it is felt,
that the whole mends only when the fragments are held.
I long for a garden, a place to plant in orange daylilies,
and see them bloom next year, but I do not work for this.

Instead I take plants in red clay pots out to catch the rain,
then set them inside where each leaf will focus the sun
like a burning green lens. I sit cross-legged on the porch
and turn my life outside in and out again, while in the pines
rain pierces the dark green needles with silver thread.
I mend the separation in my heart. I hold the heart's sorrow
and it blooms red, the courage to speak across distances,
the courage to act, like spider lilies rising unexpected
every fall, in a deserted garden, along old foundations.

1980

Gloria Anzaldúa

Tres Mujeres en el Gabinete/Three Women in the Closet

1. La mujer
que se trago
a Tonatiuh
ella de sus verijas
llueve
mares de sangre
desparama ombligos
como uvas reventadas
o ojos de venado asado.
Pavimenta
las calles consesos guisados.
Hila
postes de electricidad
con tripas de marrano capado.
Metztli
luna cara negra
mujer
que en si mismas
negamos.

1. The woman
who swallowed
Tonatiuh
rains
oceans of blood
from her genitals
scatters navels
like burst grapes or
roasted deer's eyes.
She paves
the roads with fried brains.
Threads
electric poles
with castrated pigs' guts.
Metztli
dark faced moon
woman
whom we ourselves
deny.

2. Diosa contemporanea
la mujer
que aruga
el cutis de las lagunas
peina
los arboles
con sus dientes
con ojas
barre las calles
sacude
el polvo que cubre
cuerpos
caminando
mas muertos que vivos.
Con lengua mojada
lambe
los ojos de recien nacidos.
Sus dedos

2. Contemporary goddess
the woman
who wrinkles
the flesh of the lakes
combs
the trees
with her teeth
sweeps
the trees with leaves
shakes
the dust that covers
bodies walking
more dead than alive.
With wet tongue
licks
the eyes of the newly-born.
Her fingers
tumble cars

tumban carros
desraizan mesquites
arrancan techos de casas y
cabezas de hombros de hombres.
Su respiro
empuja las vacas
colas enpiernadas a casa.
Mujer nueva,
mujer amazona.

unearth mesquites
rip
roofs from houses and
heads from the shoulders
of men.
Her breath
pushes
the cows home
tails between their legs.
New woman,
amazon woman.

3. La diosa sirvienta

Tlazolteotle
la mujer
que traga caca
y toma urines
Su piel
absorba
sudores sadisticos
deseos martisticos
pensamientos incestuosos.
Deja las almas
blancas
y de corazones
máma corajes
Tlazolteotle—la mujer que
enceramos en el ropero.

3. The servant goddess

Tlazolteotle
the woman
who swallows shit
and drinks urine
her skin
absorbs
sadistic sweat
tortured desires
incestuous thoughts.
She leaves souls
white
and from hearts
sucks anger.
Tlazolteotle
the woman
we locked
in the closet.

1978

Tonatiuh—Aztec earth goddess, sometimes synonymous with the Virgen de la Guadalupe.
Metztli—Aztec moon goddess.
Tlazolteotle—Aztec goddess of witchcraft.

—G.A.

Translation by Mary Margaret Nàvar and Nancy Dean.

Michelle Cliff

Obsolete Geography

1.

Airplane shadows moved across the mountains; leaving me to clear rivers, dancing birds, sweet fruits. Sitting on a river rock, my legs dangle in the water. I am twelve—and solitary.

2.

On a hillside I search for mangoes. As I shake the tree the fruit drops: its sweetness splits at my feet. I suck the remaining flesh from the hairy seed. The sap from the stem stains my lips: to fester later. I am warned I may be scarred.

3.

My other life of notebooks, lessons, homework continues. I try not to pay it mind.

4.

Things that live here: star apple, pineapple, custard apple, south sea apple; tamarind, ginep, avocado, guava, cashew, cane; yellow, white, St. Vincent yam; red, black, pepper ants; bats, scorpions, nightingales, spiders; cassava, sweetsop, soursop, cho-cho, okra, guango, mahoe, mahogany, ackee, plantain, chinese banana; poly lizard, green lizard, croaking lizard, ground lizard.

5.

The pig is big, and hangs suspended by her hind legs from a tree in the yard. She is screaming—her agony not self-conscious. I have been told not to watch her slaughter, but my twelve-year-old self longs for the flow of blood. A small knife is inserted in her throat, pulled back and forth; until the throat slits, the wound widens, and blood runs over, covering the yard.

As her cries cease, mine begin. I have seen other slaughters but this one will stay with me.

6.

My grandmother's verandah before they renovated the house sloped downhill. The direction the marbles took as they rolled toward the set-up dominoes was always the same. There was a particular lizard at one end, who crawled up to take the sun in the afternoon. I provoked him—knowing he had a temper, since half his tail was missing. As he got angry he turned black with rage and blew a balloon of flesh from his throat—and sat there.

7.

Sitting in the maid's room asking her about her daughter, who is somewhere else. I examine the contents of her dressing table: perfume, comb, hand-mirror, romantic comics, missal.

The maid is sunning rectangles of white cloth on the bushes behind the house. I ask her what they are. She mutters something and moves off. They are bright with whiteness and soft to the touch. I suspect they are a private matter and ask no more about them.

8.

The river—as I know it—runs from a dam at my cousins' sugar mill down to a pool at the bottom.

On Monday the women make their way to the river; balancing zinc washtubs on a braided cloth on their heads—this cloth has an African name. They take their places at specific rocks and rub, beat, wet, wring, and spread their laundry in the sun. And then leave. The rocks are streaked white after their chore is finished.

This is *our* land, *our* river—I have been told. So when women wash their clothes above the place where I swim; when the butcher's wife cleans tripe on Saturday morning; when a group of boys I do not know are using *my* pool—I hate them for taking up *my* space.

I hate them for taking up space; I hate them for not including me.

9.

The butcher's wife—after she has cleaned the tripe—comes to wax the parlor floor. She has a daughter my age who today is embarrassed and angry: I think it is because she is wearing one of my old dresses.

(Twenty years later I find she is part of us: "from" my great-uncle.)

There are many mysterious births here:

Three people come up to the steps and ask for my grandfather (who by this time is almost dead)—I am suspicious and question them closely. My grandmother explains: "They are your grandfather's *outside* children."

10.

Three women—sisters, my second cousins; unmarried; middle-aged—live across the river. They have a plant called "Midnight Mystery" on their verandah. They come late one night to fetch me and we walk down the path, our way lit by a small boy with a bottle lamp. We balance ourselves across the river and reach the house—in time to see the large white flower unfold.

11.

One reason the parlor floor is waxed on Saturday is that my grandmother holds church on Sunday. People arrive at nine and sit for two hours: giving testimony, singing hymns, reading scripture. They sip South African wine and eat squares of white bread.

Religion looms: Zinc roofs rock on Sunday morning.

12.

The river "comes down": the dam breaks; rocks shift; animals are carried along.

The clouds build across the mountains and move into our valley. Then it rains. Over the rain I can hear the noise of the river. It *is* a roar; even the gully, which pays the river tribute, roars—and becomes dangerous.

This is clear power.

13.

We cook on a woodstove in a kitchen behind the house. Our water is taken from the river in brimming kerosene tins. We read by lamp and moon light.

14.

On one hillside next to the house is the coffee piece: the bushes are low, with dark-green leaves and dark-red fruit. Darkness informs the place. Darkness and damp. Tall trees preserve the dark. Things hide here.

I pick coffee for my grandmother. To be gentle is important: the bushes are sensitive. I carefully fill my basket with the fruit.

15.

After the birth of each of my grandmother's five children the cord was buried and orange trees planted near the house. These trees now bear the names of her children.

16.

One child died—a son, at eighteen. His grave is in the flower garden, shaded by the orange trees. She tends the grave often, singing "What a Friend We Have in Jesus."

The walls of my grandmother's parlor are decorated with two photographs: of her two remaining sons.

17.

My mother is my grandmother's daughter. My acquaintance with my mother in this house is from the schoolbooks stored in boxes underneath. Worms have tunneled the pages, the covers are crossed with mold—making the books appear ancient. She has left me to find her here, under this house: I seek identity in a childish hand and obsolete geography.

18.

A madwoman steals my grandfather's horse and tries to ride away. I know several madwomen here. She is the boldest; riding bareback, naked. The others walk up and down, talking to themselves and others. One talks to a lizard in the cashew tree at the bottom of the yard. Another sits in the river, refusing to cross.

This woman—one of my cousins—tells me twenty years later about her terror of leaving her place; about the shock treatments the family arranges in town; about how she kept the accounts; about her sister's slow death and how she cared for her.

It must have meant something that all those mad were women. The men were called idiots (an accident of birth); or drunks.

The women's madness was ascribed to several causes: childlessness, celibacy, "change": such was the nature of their naive science.

19.

An old woman who sometimes works for us has built a house by the roadside. It is built of clay—from the roadbed—with wood for structure. It has a thatch roof and rests on cement blocks. It is one-room.

She promises to make me a cake if I help her paper the walls. I arrive early, my arms filled with newspapers. We mix flour paste and seek suitable stories for decoration. Pleased with our results, we gather flowers and put them in gourds around the room. True to her word, she bakes me a cake in an empty condensed milk tin.

20.

Walking down to the shop by the railway crossing, saying good morning, people stop me and ask for my mother—often mistaking me for her.

21.

I want to visit my mother's school where she broke her ankle playing cricket and used the books which now lie under the house. I can't get to the school but I play cricket; using a carved bamboo root as she did and the dried stalk of a coconut tree for a bat. I play on the same pitch she used—a flat protected place across the road.

22.

Walking through the water and over the rocks, I am exploring the river—eating bitter susumba and sweet valencia oranges. Up past pools named for people who drowned there; to the dam; to the sugar mill where I get wet sugar.

23.

What is here for me: where do these things lead:
warmth
light
wet sugar
rain and river water
earth
the wood fire
distance
slaughter
mysterious births
fertility
the women at the river
my grandmother's authority with land and scripture
a tree named with my mother's name.

Twenty years later these things rush back at me: the memories of a child inside and outside.

24.

Behind the warmth and light are dark and damp/behind the wet sugar, cane fields/behind the rain and river water, periods of drought/underneath the earth are the dead/underneath the wood fire are ashes to be emptied/underneath the distance is separation/underneath the slaughter is hunger/behind the mysterious births is my own/behind the fertility are the verdicts of insanity/behind the women at the river are earlier women/underlying my grandmother's authority with land and scripture is obedience to a drunken husband/under a tree named with my mother's name is a rotted cord.

1978

Barbara Smith

Theft

for Angelina Weld Grimké

The white women
are talking about
their poets.

For hours.

While claiming that
they do not have enough.

I gather strength and
throw my voice into
the world
they think they know.

Tell them,

Yes.

There were some few
Black women
who wrote
and lived their lives
loving women.

They are curious.

But when I say
the Black namesake
of someone white
they think they know

One shouts:

"She's not Black!"

Teeth clenching
I try to explain in seconds

about bloodlines,
Black and white halves of families.
Rape.
Refight for her convenience
the Civil War.
Finally her slender arrogance
is still.

That night
I look for comfort
in the poet,
whose life was crushed
by everything she was,
including Black.

She merely warns me
in a hidden tongue
that for survival
we must often play invisible,
the Masquerade,
must save our best and
darkest selves for us.

1977

Grimkē was named in memory of her great-aunt, Angelina Grimkē Weld, a white abolitionist and advocate of women's rights. Also see "Introduction."

Wilmette Brown

Bushpaths

the road is strewn with fallen wings
and the stench of mangled dogs
follows frightened barefoot travelers on the sidetracks
cattle scatter on burning hoofs
to escape the blast of horns
and faded women sell subsistence cobs
and watermelons along the highway

africa
who scratched these roads
in pitch
across your face
new scars
to mark the new maturity
the knowledge of imperial evil
for surely
these are the paths of plunder
that violate the sacred forests
to race for hidden treasures
leaving us
a continent of opened secrets

they are not our roads
that trample through the maize field
and cramp the lion in her kingdom
that steal across whole villages
and parcel out the continent
into national thoroughfares
to deliver the goods
to europe

1972

Voices from the Diaspora Home

we would have perished in the sea
but it was cool in the sea beneath the sun
so we swelled into each other in the sea
and flowered into islands
flowering new people
same old need to be

and we too will build africa
if not in africa
then from the bottom of the sea
we will scatter
black pearls from shore to shore
for scattering does not destroy the seed

distillation of the teeming niger
and of the flaming seas of zanj
we kept the drums alive
from four continents
they called back to you
in tunes we did not know
we remembered
we blew into borrowed skins and wires and reeds
the same rhythms in new tongues
to mardi gras we carried the marimba
and pounded out songs at christmas
on the plantations of maryland
like washing our hands in the river juba
and they were not the songs of botswana
the songs of ghana
or zanzibar
they were africa's songs
to which we now
like an echo
are returning

but the people are shouting anthems
orchestrated in berlin
and we with our songs are applauded
like wandering minstrels
outside the people's chorus

but we too will build africa
if not in africa
then from the bottom of the sea
we will scatter
black pearls from shore to shore
for scattering does not destroy the seed

1975

Cheryl Clarke

Palm-Reading

To soften the terror of living
the old black witch does not tell me everything at once.
She withholds the unwholesome forecast.
It catches in her throat
and dissolves into a telling of the ravaged past:

"Dissected trees, dismantled houses, vi-o-lated genitals."

'This I know. I know this.'

"Crowded crossings, unwelcomed landings, forced, futile toil."

'I know all this from before. Something more.'

"The pillage of the soul!"

'Go deeper.'

"Inspite of the mutilations, the vibrations is very strong. And . . . there is yet some grace for the future."

The old black witch keeps her sources well,
and does not tell me everything at once.
Holds back the unwholesome forecast.
Re-tells the ravaged past.
Closes her misty eyes to the lines,
tightens her fist against her teeth,
draws in her breath,
gives me back my hand.
And does not tell me everything at once.

1976

Freedom Flesh

for Assata Shakur

had you not chosen the dangerous business of freedom,
you could be walking barefoot in the red hills of north carolina
hand-in-hand with kakuya
instead of assuming disguises and aliases
and traveling through subway stations
and camping in sacred aboriginal territory
you could have been a school marm
a graduate student
a community organizer
instead of an underground railroad conductor
whose picture can be seen in post offices
or on some hastily-drafted poster advertising
liberation

you could have continued giving yourself guitar lessons
writing political poems
you could have become a public speaker
instead of an ex-political prisoner
a paradox an irony a phenomenon
the flesh of freedom

1980

Alice Bloch

Six Years

for Nancy

A friend calls us
an old married couple

I flinch
you don't mind
On the way home
you ask why I got upset
We are something
like what she said
you say   I say
No

We aren't married
No one has blessed
this union   no one
gave us kitchen gadgets
We bought our own blender
We build our common life
in the space between the laws

Six years
What drew us together
a cartographer   a magnetic force
our bodies   our speech
the wind   a hunger

Listeners both
we talked

I wanted: your lean wired energy
control   decisiveness
honesty   your past
as an athlete

You wanted:
my "culture"
gentleness   warmth

Of course that was doomed
You brought out
my anger   I resist
your control   your energy
exhausts me   my hands
are too hot for you   you gained
the weight I lost   my gentleness
is dishonest   your honesty
is cruel   you hate
my reading   I hate
your motorcycle

Yet something has changed
You have become gentler
I more decisive
We walk easily
around our house
into each other's language
There is nothing
we cannot say together

Solid ground
under our feet
we know this landscape
We have no choice
of destination   only the route
is a mystery   every day
a new map of the same terrain

1978

Karen Brodine

The Receptionist Is by Definition

her personal life has very little to do with
this grim determination. telephone lines constrict
her arms and legs.
        1. the receptionist is by definition
                always interruptable.

she cut two people off today in one punch
of the button. the pencil is hooked with
string to the phone so no one can walk off
                with her.

'will you hold please? I'll see if he's in.'
(are you in?)
'I'm sorry, sir, he's out.'
        2. the receptionist is by definition under-
                paid to lie.

remember the receptionist with the lovely
smile, with the green eyes, the cropped
hair, big feet, small knees, with the
wrinkled hands, the large breasts, with
the husky voice, the strong chin?
        she takes her breaks
in the washroom, grimacing, waving her fists
at the blurred reflection of her dress.

1976

Making the Difference

1.
ever since I found out I was hired to teach a class,
my words have been reversing. seascape becomes scapesea
cashing a check, checking a cash. I walk backwards
into the blackboard, waving. my words come out like
reading someone's newspaper on the bus, sneaky, at an angle.

we were talking about death but we were really talking about
feeling powerless. though my mother said once she dreamt dying
was like flying off a cliff, perfectly sure.

my grandma wants hershey bars. her feet don't touch the floor
in the nursing home chair. her car, newly equipped with power
steering, sits in the driveway covered with leaves. I am afraid
to see her. I am afraid she will look up at me and ask
for a hershey bar.

2.

difficult Monday. Rosemary fired. could have been any of us.
I see the cracked window in the boss's office. a brick?
John Ng says, no, a window-washer did it, months ago.
we are all touchy about voice-tones, looks. who will join us?
the postman who cleans here on his lunch-hour says, 'what's
going on? how come it's so quiet around here?' the union
notice is posted by the sink and everyone stares at the cups.
John C. says *he* doesn't want to pay dues. Ike raises his eyebrows
and grins at me. the big and little bosses try to keep track.
little boss Ken watches over my shoulder while I do opaquing work.
I keep my hand steady and ignore him. two of the machines
break down. I lose a strip of type in the waxer. what next?
I try to decide how to get home, which combination of buses.
the bart train stops in the tunnel, crowded. the doors open,
close, open, close. people lurch in one direction as it moves forward,
then, as a body, right themselves.

3.

my grandmother grips my hands as if they were truth and
calls me 'Mary, Mary!' my mother's name.

at work we say we will vote yes, and then over the days,
some faces seem fearful, not sure. I try to be strong,
every minute, and sure, but I want to take a rest,
go to sleep, just for an hour.

when I tell Kim of a friend who began to cry, I say,
'she is so vulnerable, her pain waits to spill over,'
and right there in the cafeteria, a man stacking chairs
on the tables around us, I want to cry too.

grandma was in too much pain to know me. I stood there
and looked out the hospital window. I had dreamt of a ghost
in a black coat, now I felt like an old coat thrown over the chair.
I look out and the bay wasn't beautiful and it wasn't ugly.
It was just there, flat and blue, with its edge of industry.
and every bone in her face distinct as scaffolding.

'can't you take it away Mary?' grandma says, 'can't you just
take it and put it outside the house?'

'no, I can't take the pain away, I'm sorry.'

'all we can hope' my mother says later, 'all we can hope
is a quick end, not to linger.'

in two weeks we will have a union election. we will vote yes and no.
we will win or lose. it will make a difference. in two weeks
she may be even thinner. if she is alive, her hands will grip
a nurse's hands. if she is alive, her hands will beat against my dreams,
all pulse, all assertion.

1977

Ellen Marie Bissert

Groves II

i called you
because i became frightened
& needed you
to dance with me
to press like flower petals the tiny bones of your back with my palms
tonight
i know you are sleeping with her
& wonder if she could hold you as tightly against the hardness
of still white stars
as i
who cannot be jealous
but for the full moon & the long night
i have to share

1972

A Romance

romeo couldn't come
& god is a stupid ass with a limpleaking prick
that's why I need to be some poet
i never got invited to the prom
but got hot on Nothingness & did the polka with my dog
i blame my tubercular father who died before he could remember my name
my married lovers who could've loved me if i looked beautiful
& my monkey-faced analyst who needed me to be screwed
i don't give a shit if sperm freezes over
i'll die alone & dig it
loving a woman in a black leather jacket
& walking into The Duchess with my polka-dot tie & lace shirt
this is my life & i now ask everyone to dance.

1973

Farewell

so what life is hard, bitter & sad
i can't make it my business
i'm not Sappho
i can't let the sun burn out my heart
i want to be alone & free
i want to be the girl dancing her life away on Bandstand
this week
i ached so dancing with the women i held in my arms
i could not write poems
now the days are long & the windows open
green rain rushes thru
wet wind
why does the whiteness of my body still turn out to her

1973

ode to my true nature

> *. . . It is conceivable that the forceful suppression of women's inordinate sexual demands was a prerequisite to the dawn of every modern civilization and almost every living culture. Primitive woman's sexual drive was too strong, too susceptible to the fluctuating extremes of an impelling, aggressive eroticism to withstand the disciplined requirements of a settled family life . . . .*
> —Mary Jane Sherfey, *The Nature and Evolution of Female Sexuality**

i can't get anything done on time
i have 10 lovers
i am writing 3 novels
& a treatise on orgies in medieval convents
so lazy
i sleep & dream on anything that transports me
trucks that haul thousands of my best-selling poems
giant slides that slip me into caressing pools of bubbling water
railroad cars that dump matriarchal sex rites into the Sistine Chapel

i have always known myself
to be sacred
virgin

insatiable in satiation
capable of more than 50 orgasms in an hour
like mermaids wanton in silvery caves
like the qadishtu of Babylonia, Sumeria, Lydia
like the priestesses of Corinth, Crete, Lesbos, Egypt
orgiastic in temples, baths, & menstrual huts
women orgasmic in beauty parlors, sororities, & ladies' rooms
ishtaritu
witch
nun
lesbian
shrew
infused with the brilliance of my bleeding fertility
i drip with holy silken fluid
for myself   for other women

a menace to civilization
i cannot be trusted
i cannot be trusted with your children
your tender nubile daughters
i cannot be trusted
to perpetuate your sons
your giant dark mushrooms in the sky

1980

See Helen Diner's Mothers and Amazons, *Elizabeth Gould Davis's* The First Sex, *and Merlin Stone's* When God Was a Woman *for a more balanced view.*
virgin—Meant in the matriarchal sense—an unmarried woman, not necessarily without knowledge of sex, in control of her sexuality, her self.
qadishtu—Akkadian word referring to priestesses who performed sacred sexual rites in the temple of the Goddess.
ishtaritu—Akkadian word referring to the priestess of Ishtar.

—*E. M. B.*

Esther Silverman

South Bronx Girl

in memory of Debbie's sister

que le pegaron tres tiros
what am I to say
that she was too young a girl
that it happens
once too often and I am sorry
that time may numb the nerves
with tilo leaves forgotten
and seal the case anyway
though she has no name
in the obituaries
that save a space
for all the Park Avenue
cardiac arrests
you tell me now
what am I to say   tell me
cause I have no
high sounding words
no eulogies
for my South Bronx girl
and this is definitely
a South Bronx death
buried in the debris
with three shots in her head
another casualty
of the streets
what words can be inscribed
on her grave
Pedro sucks cock and
Manuel was here 110th
no you bring your prayers
for I have nothing to say
bring your botanica candles
burnt out butts and broken glass
but please no flowers
for this latina that lies here

1979

que le pegaron tres tiros (Spanish)—She was shot three times.

Becky Birtha

At 20, I began to know
I wanted to grow
Up to be a woman.
Sensed the power in that word
Woman like no one I knew
to look up to

At 23 I stood in a city field
And reeled out 700 feet of string–
Take a good look–
You've never seen
Anyone like this before
Nor will you soon again–
    brown-skinned woman
    in a long skirt
    her kite flying higher
    than any of the men–

At the poetry workshop
I'm the woman across the room from you
Take it in:
    she's in a soft pink peasant shirt
    under her overalls
    pinned in the center pocket
    that symbol for women loving women
    print kerchief tied behind
    brown face, brown eyes intent
    on the woman who's speaking
    drinking it in, saying yes
    while her fingers never stop
    knitting a small blue mitten
    the size of a little girl's hand
I look up to
All your lovely faces watching me
Yes, I am exactly what you see
My card is strength.
I am the woman I always wanted to be.

1976

Alison Colbert

The White Worm

1.
The body of a young guerrilla
is flung into a ravine in the Philippines
overhung with green vines and red hibiscus.

The covert man goes to the screened compound,
calls the overt man, who calls a mother
in D.C. who is the highest-ranking
woman in the C.I.A.
He says, "Area pacified."

She does not know about the body.

2.
In New York
the breast of her daughter
is cut open
is sectioned like an orange.
The flap of skin hangs loosely.

3.
The brother of the woman
with the cut breast
lies in his coffin.
A white worm crawls out
of his eyes.
The Austin Healy he died under
is rusting in a ditch
in a dump.

4.
The father and mother of the son
in the grave and the daughter with
the cut breast are sitting at breakfast
in a light dining room
eating toast and eggs kept warm

on a Salton Hottray.
They fight about which of them
brought up their son
to drive drunk and
crush himself under a car.
Each thinks, "You killed him,"
and they swallow their eggs.

The curtains move in the breeze.
The dust collects on their books.
The Filipino rots in the ditch.

5.
The covert man is sitting on a
screened veranda
surrounded by red hibiscus
reading *The Spy Who Came in From the Cold.*
He stops to write a letter of condolence
to the mother.

6.
The mother, the highest-ranking woman
in the C.I.A., is typing the footnotes for her
book on the Vietnam War.

Her daughter is writing the draft of a poem
about her cut breast.

She does not know about the body.

7.
Her father and mother will pay
for the silver knife that cuts
her breast.
Her mother gets a green check
on Thursday from the feds
and deposits it in the gray crypt
of the bank.

The hospital gets a check in the mail.

8.
The Filipino is rotting in a ditch
under a tangle of weeds and hibiscus.
A white worm crawls out of his eyes.

The mother gets another green check
and goes out to buy eggs.

The tumor has been cut out.
The area has been pacified.

The knife cuts through the flower
of the tit.

The flower rots in the ditch
of the grave.

1975

Susan Saxe

Notes from the First Year

for my sisters, a trilogy of revolution

1. Patience

There is no need now to rush about my life,
I have time, each day, to unfold
carefully, my rage–
no longer impotent,
But the most powerful force in the universe.
(Do you hear me, Mother?)
Slowly like a sunflower, like a tree,
Revolution unfolds before me:
Newspaper pages beginning with world news,
and ending with the comics,
and classified ads announcing the end
of things as we know them.
Inevitably the world, the nation, the city,
    the arts, society, sports
and personals
will be recycled
By patient origamists, armed with love.

2. Questionnaire

There is unfeminine (but oh, so Female)
sureness in my hands,
checking "No." to every question
in the Harris poll, Reader's Digest,
    Mademoiselle,
I am an outlaw, so none of that applies to me:
I do not vote in primaries, do not wish to increase
    my spending power, do not take birth control
    pills.
I do not have a legal residence, cannot tell you
    my given name or how (sometimes very) old
    I really am.
I do not travel abroad, see no humor in uniforms,
    and my lips are good enough for my lover
    as they are.
Beyond that, no one heads my household, I would not

save my marriage if I had one, or anybody else's
if I could.
I do not believe that politicians need me, that Jesus
loves me, or that short men are particularly sexy.
Nor do I want a penis.
What else do you have to offer?

3. I Argue My Case

Gentlemen of the Jury:
I have had the time and opportunity to appear
before you in the guise
(disguise) of every woman:
to you, sir, I was the dumb hand
that wiped your
table,
to you, sir, a flimsy black
skirt on legs,
to you, some hard
down-on-me woman who might
(or might not) yet
be downed again.
To him, an ass,
to him, a breast, a leg
to him.
To that one, just another working bitch.
To each, another history, to each
another (partial) lie.
We women are liars, you say.
(It is written.)
But you have made us so.
We are too much caught up in cycles, you say.
But your gods cannot prevent that.
So we act out our cycles,
one or many,
in the rhythm of what has to be
(because we say so)
our common destiny.
And so, before you are taken in by one of our
perfect circles,
remember also that we are in perfect
motion.
And when you (and you will)

run counter to the flow of revolution,
the wheel of women will continue to turn,
and grind you
so fine

1970

Dorothy Allison

Boston, Massachusetts

Boston, Massachusetts, three years ago.
A woman told me about a woman dead,
a woman who might not have been known to be a lesbian.

No one is sure they knew that. The cops didn't say that.
They said she was wearing a leather jacket, blue jeans, old boots,
said she had dark cropped hair and was new to the neighborhood,
living in an old brick rowhouse with three other women.
They said she was carrying a can of gasoline. They did not say why,
if it was a car waiting or a jar of sticky brushes.
They said she was white, that her friends were white,
that the neighborhood was bad, that she and her friends were fools,
didn't belong there, were queer anyway.
They said the young rough crowd of men laughed a lot
when they stopped her,
that she laughed back,
and then they made her pour the gasoline over her own head.

Later some cop said she was a hell of a tough bitch,
'cause she walked two blocks on her own feet,
two blocks to the all-night grocery where another little crowd watched
going "SHIIIIIIIT!"
"Will you look at that?"
"Look at that."

I read about it in the paper—two paragraphs.
I have carried that story with me since, wanting more,
wanting no woman to be two such stark paragraphs.

We become our deaths.
Our names disappear and our lovers leave town,
heartbroken, crazy.
But we are the ones who die.
We are the forgotten
burning in the streets
hands out, screaming,
"This is not all I am.
I had something else in mind to do."

Not on that street,
screaming,
always and only that,
where there was so much so much more she had to do.

Sometimes when I love my lover,
        I taste in my mouth
        ashes
        gritty
        grainy
grating between the teeth
the teeth of a woman
probably known to be a lesbian.

1979

Olga Broumas

the knife & the bread

for the women of Cyprus, '74

in the morning
the room is sharp with mirrors
the light is helpless

i skirt
your livewire laughter
i embrace the wall, fat curtains bellying
in on the wind: cooler weather

i tell you violence
perseveres, the light being cruel
itself
to the beveled edges
i look, i cannot forget
though i flap my mind like a breathless tongue

o

i am sick with knives, knives
slashing breasts away, hand-held
knives cutting wounds to be raped
by cocks, thick blunt knives
sheathing blood, knives
paring cheeks away
knives
in the belly
apples won't comfort me
this isn't love

this dance i pant from not safe
or ancient, its steps
marred with the fall of women
falling
from cliffs, walls, anything
to escape this war
without national

boundary, this fear
beyond tribes

o

you, over there, dark
as a church, insular
can ignore the light
in the cruel mirrors

you laugh/ a knife
in your
belly would
slice only guts

o

when the enemy comes
the men run to the mountains

they are rebels
they sing to their knives
wash out their hair & prepare themselves
for a manly death

young women hide in the cellars

old women wait

when the enemy comes
they make the old women dance
make them sing/ underground
an infant begins to wail
in her single knowledge

the old ones sing louder
dance faster, fit these new words
to their frenzied song: *daughter, oh*
throttle her
or slaughter her
or gag her on your breast

you have seen their breasts

rolling in mounds, little pyramids
in the soldiers' wake

o

i slice the bread
in the kitchen, i hold the knife

steady against the grain
that feeds us
all
indiscriminate
as an act of god

i hold the knife
& i slice the bread/ the west
light low on the blade
liquid, exhausted
the food

chaste on the table & powerless
to contain us, how long
can i keep the knife

in its place

1974

Amazon Twins

1.
You wanted to compare, and there
we were, eyes on each eye, the lower
lids
squinting
suddenly awake

though the light was dim. Looking away
some time ago, you'd said
the eyes are live
animals, domiciled in our head
but more than the head

is crustacean-like. Marine
eyes, marine
odors. Everything live
(tongue, clitoris, lip and lip)
swells in its moist shell. I remember the light

warped round our bodies finally
crustal, striated with sweat.

2.
In the gazebo-like café, you gave
me food from your plate, alert
to my blood-sweet hungers
double-edged
in the glare of the sun's
and our own
twin heat. Yes, there

we were, breasts on each side, Amazons
adolescent at twentynine
privileged
to keep the bulbs and to feel the blade
swell, breath-sharp
on either side. In that public place

in that public place.

1975

Artemis

Let's not have tea. White wine
eases the mind along
the slopes
of the faithful body, helps

any memory once engraved
on the twin
chromosome ribbons, emerge, tentative
from the archaeology of an excised past.

I am a woman

who understands
the necessity of an impulse whose goal or origin
still lies beyond me. I keep the goat

for more
than the pastoral reasons. I work
in silver the tongue-like forms
that curve round a throat

an arm-pit, the upper
thigh, whose significance stirs in me
like a curviform alphabet
that defies

decoding, appears
to consist of vowels, beginning with O, the O-
mega, horseshoe, the cave of sound.
What tiny fragments

survive, mangled into our language.
I am a woman committed to
a politics
of transliteration, the methodology

of a mind
stunned at the suddenly
possible shifts of meaning—for which
like amnesiacs

in a ward on fire, we must
find words
or burn.

1975

Sometimes, as a child

when the Greek sea
was exceptionally calm
the sun not so much a pinnacle
as a perspiration of light, your brow and the sky
meeting on the horizon, sometimes

you'd dive
from the float, the pier, the stone
promontory, through water so startled
it held the shape of your plunge, and there

in the arrested heat of the afternoon
without thought, effortless
as a mantra turning
you'd turn
in the paused wake of your dive, enter
the suck of the parted waters, you'd emerge

clean caesarean, flinging
live rivulets from your hair, your own
breath arrested. Something immaculate, a chance

crucial junction: time, light, water
had occurred, you could feel your bones
glisten
translucent as spinal fins.
                                        In rain-
green Oregon now, approaching thirty, sometimes

the same
rare concert of light and spine
resonates in my bones, as glistening
starfish, lover, your fingers
beach up.

1976

Sleeping Beauty

I sleep, I sleep
too long, sheer hours
hound me, out
of bed and into clothes, I wake
still later, breathless, heart
racing, sleep
peeling off like a hairless
glutton, momentarily
slaked. Cold

water shocks me
back from the dream. I see
lovebites like fossils: *something*
that did exist

dreamlike, though
dreams have the perfect alibi, no
fingerprints, evidence
that a mirror could float
back in your own face, gleaming
its silver eye. Lovebites like fossils. Evidence.
Strewn

round my neck like a ceremonial
necklace, suddenly
snapped apart.

o

Blood. Tears. The vital
salt of our body. Each
other's mouth.
Dreamlike

the taste of you
sharpens my tongue like a thousand shells,
bitter, metallic. I know

as I sleep
that my blood runs clear
as salt
in your mouth, my eyes.

o

City-center, mid-
traffic, I
wake to your public kiss. Your name
is Judith, your kiss a sign

to the shocked pedestrians, gathered
beneath the light that means
stop
in our culture

where red is a warning, and men
threaten each other with final violence: *I will drink*
your blood. Your kiss
is for them

a sign of betrayal, your red
lips suspect, unspeakable
liberties as
we cross the street, kissing
against the light, singing, *This*
is the woman I woke from sleep, the woman that woke
me sleeping.

1976

There are people who do not explore the in-
Sides of flowers . . .
—Sandra Hochman

With the clear
plastic speculum, transparent
and when inserted, pink like the convex
carapace of a prawn, flashlight in hand, I
guide you
inside the small
cathedral of my cunt. The unexpected
light dazzles you. This flesh, my darling, always
invisible like the wet
side of stones, the hidden
hemisphere of the moon, startles you
with its brilliance, the little
dome a spitting
miniature of the Haghia Sophia
with its circlet of openings
to the Mediterranean Sun.
A woman-made language would
have as many synonyms for pink/light-filled/holy as
the Eskimo does
for snow. Speechless, you
shift the flashlight from
hand to hand, flickering. An orgy
of candles. Lourdes in mid-August. A flurry of

audible breaths, a seething
of holiness, and
behold
a tear
forms in the single eye, carmine
and catholic. You too, my darling, are
folded, clean
round a light-filled temple, complete
with miraculous icon, shedding
her perfect tears, in touch
with the hidden hemispheres
the dome
of our cyclops moon.

1976

Haghia Sophia—Byzantine church, Istanbul, built in the 6th Century A.D. by Justinian. The dome, covered with gold tesserae, floats on a rim of 40 windows encircling its base.

Lorraine Sutton

Your Olive Face

your olive face appears before me
in the quiet of night.

i think of you, your life, real
surreal.

i think of your everyday rituals,
uncomplicated routine.

i think of your few hours sleep
where you escape the drudgery
for awhile.

i think of your dreams
    three ring circuses.
    last year's memories.
    elephants/asses
    treading water past
    the gate.

i feel the waves of your invisible
beats.

i feel the rhythms of your Attica
Viet Nam/Chile/Boston/pounding
inside my bed.

i feel the colors, your violent
shades of colors dripping down
my thighs.

i feel your tremble contain the
dance of all the wooden soldiers:
Army/Navy/Police/Marines/quick
&
hard
you contain them all.

i see your sleeping face before me

look as if you have never felt the
waves/nor seen the lights/not even
shades of lights that bounce across
the world.

i think of your few hours sleep
where you escape the drudgery for
awhile/where you can escape today

but

not tomorrow.

1972

Ruthe D. Canter

The Resemblance

My mother and I
bear resemblance.
One eye at a time,
one eye and we
are one. Our breasts
are silences that
meet each other in
a grace. Hands, our
hands like pockets
of tiny grains, scattering
in and out of lines
the markings of
resemblance.

I am strong like your
torso, you are strong
like my neck. Our
sorrows sit behind our
eyes like unborn children;
our sorrows, our hymns.

I am sad, I am singing,
my breasts become like
yours, my hands with
the same lines, I am
singing for the mother
whose sorrows I am.

1974

Jan Clausen

likeness

but with you, also, i would want it.
forget what you learned, the sums
of your arduous schooling.
that is all labor, making something,
the grass grow where it never grew before;
that is capitalism, industry, hard pleasure
consuming the planet,
prodigious and admirable work.

this is love in the mirror. the light
girdles the galaxies and falls right back.
the dark star, kleptomaniac, absorbs.
this is only the world's most natural act

and though i know your body by my own
i need to fit my disembodied hands
around the difficult answers of your bones
and want to float you always when i plunge
all the way down
to tongue you into darkly grieving waves,
not of the sea-kind, but more resonant ones.

see, i can swim, can dance, can mourn
can open   my book   my body
my eyes for you under water.

1974

SESTINA, WINCHELL'S DONUT HOUSE

Watching the black hours through to morning
I'd set out each successive tray of grease-
cooked donuts on the rack, chocolate and pink-
frosted, to harden beneath the fluorescent light,
talk to crazy Harry, count the change,
listen to top-forty radio. Mostly, I was alone.

Every stranger's suspect when you're alone.
A woman was beaten badly early one morning
by a man who sneaked in the back while she made change,
so I'd rehearse scenarios of scooping grease,
flinging it at the assailant's face, cooking the light
or dark flesh to curl away at the impact, angry pink.

The cab drivers came in every night, faces polished pink
and boyish, arriving in pairs or alone.
Their cabs clotted like moths at the building's light.
They were outlaws and brothers, despised men who rise in the morning.
They'd swagger, still dapper, if fattened on sweets and grease,
call me sugar and honey. I smiled. I kept the change.

Often I was too busy to see the darkness change,
flush from black to blue to early pink.
At four o'clock, my face smeared with congealed grease,
I think I was happiest, although most alone.
The harder hours were those of fullblown morning,
fighting depression, sleeping alone in the light.

Linda came in at six, awash with light,
businesslike, making sure there'd be enough change
to get her through the rigors of the morning.
She had a hundred uniforms; I remember pink.
Sometimes she'd cheat, leave me to work alone,
sneak out to flirt in parked cars, fleeing lifetimes of grease.

I can see her cranking the hopper, measuring grease,
indefatigable, wired on coffee, just stopping to light
her cigarettes. She didn't want to be alone.
It was only my fantasy that she could change,
stop wearing that silly, becoming pink,
burn free of the accidents, husband and children, some morning.

I remember walking home those mornings, smelling of grease,
amazed in summer's most delicate pink early light,
to shower, change, and sleep out the hot day alone.

1974

dialectics

Outside and inside are just an illusion.
—Assata Shakur, "What Is Left?"

1.
scarlike, the continent
puckers, drawn together
by dreams, by what
i remember: the bulk
of land traversed
to get here, not
in airplanes, unreal,
but actually, on roads

and even winter wearies
and ice breaks up
on the river
piss-yellow sun
soaks through the haze
above Flatbush
cells poise to divide
the first forced crocuses
choke the florist's shop

too long i have been
floating, dreaming
mountains, the future
safe like money
in the bank, a lack
of limits, fistful
of lottery tickets
dreaming (what's wrong
with this picture?)
i am the exception

you can be anything
is what they taught me
down the road apiece
i caught them in their lie
i have known the odd half-life
of the emigree
wintering on the fat
of the old regime

scraping the privilege, bitter
from my plate

i'm what
i have
to hate
white skin
and history

2. (Assata on trial in New Jersey)
contradictions, ice cream
at the demo, a beautiful
day in New Brunswick,
picket fences, black cops,
neat red brick jail, that
all-white jury

we shout around the courthouse
free to leave
to take the bus
be someone else in the city

and never yet for us
the patient faces
that watch the prosecutor
know they can do this

and never the handcuffs
and never the sun denied
and never the muscles destroyed
and never the love postponed
and never the life abridged
and never the isolation
articulated in concrete
and never the testing
never the testing of limits
and never New Jersey's
obliterating eyes

and never anything irrevocable

and never the headlines:
CHESIMARD GUILTY OF MURDER

3. (the road)
spring comes late to these
upthrust slabs
of granite
evergreens sheltering
rotten snow

maples bud red
in the hollows
it is raining
onto rock, onto elms
knee-deep
in watery fields,
onto bright bulldozed
embankments, barns
falling in

to see clearly, is that
the greatest gift?

this austere country
floods me with its
narrow band of colors:
dark-layered earth
dark sky

brimming
i drive
north

4.
in childbirth
you focus on technique

how difficult
to stay awake
keep moving

like climbing Everest
without equipment
snowblind
hand over hand
up the ice face

how difficult
to live inside my story

**5. (reading Plath's *Letters Home;*
rereading *Ariel*)
i skim like a thriller
these last communiques.
the hyperactive poet
proclaims she's coping.
"I'm happier than ever."
manic. dead-ended.

and yet the release it is,
the icy comfort
after the cloying tone
of Ted and babies.
"I am a genius poet."
she knew her power,
knew images pouring,
the epileptic's aura.
hoped, for a moment,
that gift could be turned
to profit. but signed
her suicide, her QED.

nothing
is preparation
for these poems,
the mathematics,
cold unanswerable facts,
pain buffed
to the luster
of science,
impersonal art.
i will not deny
her February death.
i tell you this,
who have no use
for quitters:

the blood
jet is

self-
hatred

6. (upstate poetry tour)
i ask what lake this is.
they tell me Erie.
there are widows' walks here,
nowhere near the sea.
there's pinball
to be played
in the Greyhound station
in Rochester, ugly
under April rain

i want to talk
about these pitted
faces. the station
is the same
as any other:
mixture of sweat,
impatience, lack
of sleep. someone
with choices
would not choose
to sit here.

the word "workingclass"
doesn't say it
doesn't describe

on the bus, a woman
holding her year-old baby
six or eight hours,
rocked and cursed to sleep

how the houses
left unpainted
go downhill faster

or the snatched, furtive
pleasures, leaching
away of a life.

7.
snow in a strange city
hungry in the morning
in a cluttered room
that makes me think of Portland
i pick the book from the shelf
and read before breakfast
of the Cuban woman
who told the prison guards
If he has not talked under torture
much less will I
when they brought her
the bloody eye
of her blinded brother.
of several women
who had been prostitutes.
of one who died
disarming a faulty bomb.
of Che not come back
from the hills. of anonymous
others.

it says here
certain scars
can never heal.

8.
i am a lesbian, forfeit
the universal. i cannot
tour Cuba in comfort
nor read my poetry
to rooms with kind men in them
smiling kindly
to halls with well-
heeled poetry
lovers in them
clamoring for the truth.

9.
listen, my ancestors
rooted up stumps

from their thin-soiled farms
in northern Minnesota,
ate roots
before the first greens
could be gathered.
they knew
an immediacy of fields,
the next row of corn
to be planted.

10.
to choose a side
is only the half of it
and nothing is simple
and nothing is finished, ever
the truth is dense and shaded,
a living forest
there are no guarantees

to choose reality
is to wake in chains
on stony ground
in the ice-edged desert dawn

all things sharp-outlined
peculiarly themselves

it is to begin

1977

Sapphire

She hated the rain. Never could figure out what people be talkin' bout when they be talkin' bout gentle, refreshing, spring rains bathing the earth's surface! This nasty ass, cold, greyness pouring down combining with shit in the street sho wadn't sweet. Her wig was wet. Hairspray and rainwater mingled with perspiration and ran down her neck. Her feet were like blocks of ice. "Muthafuck this shit," she mumbled, "I'm turnin' in for the nite."

As she strolled past the likker store she looked down the street at the elementary school she usta go to wondering what her mother would say. "Well," she thot, "least I ain' on welfare." The street was deserted. At three o'clock in the mornin' Webster and Grove looked like something out of a movie. She shivered and quickened her pace. Some putty faced pig in a blue chevy slowed down and while cruising along side he leered, "Pssst wanna date? Huh honey? How bout it?" She almost ran; she couldn't have taken another feebly dick, pink, hairy son of a bitch if he'd been shittin' fifty dollar bills. She walked over to Hayes St. lo and behold—a bus—a rare occurrence at three o'clock in the morning. She hopped on the bus, sauntered to the back hopin' Willie wouldn't be upset bout her not gettin' no whole lot of money. Shit! Wet as it was the mutherfucker oughtta be glad she got what she got. She jumped off the bus and motored down the street hopin' there was some brownies left cause all night she'd been wantin' somethin' sweet. She started up the stairs, slid up to the doe and laid on the bell. No one answered. She wondered what was takin' so long. Shit! Even if no one else was in Jackie be in. She was always the first one in! Sometimes she thot that bitch had a stash cause can't nobodi come up wid that much cash every nite! "Hell," she muttered, "What's wrong wid these fools?" She laid on the bell again. Willie usually be home about this time too. Finally she heard footsteps approaching the doe. They musta been fuckin'. Still that son of a bitch didn't have to take till Christmas to answer the door. She heard him on the other side of the door . . . his footsteps . . . his breathing.

Willie opened the peephole and said, "What cha want?"

"Nigger r u crazy!" she said, "what u think I want! Lemme in!"

"How much cash u got?"

"Bout seventyfive."

"U triflin' bitch u mean u been out all nite and ain't got but seventyfive dollars? You musta been jivin' round smokin' weed wid the other bitches!"

"Willie u know better than that. I ain' lazy. It's jus been slow. Come on daddy." she wheedled, "Open the doe."

He opened the door, grabbing her left arm with his right hand, yanked her around and placed a well aimed patent leathered foot in her ass and said, "Bitch u get in when u got my money."

Enraged and scared she sobbed, "Bu . . ., But Willie its rainin'!"

Willie slammed the door, opened the peephole and tole her,

"Walk between the raindrops baby walk between the raindrops."

1973

New York City Tonight

1. I'm talkin' about
   a sickness
   inside
   A feelin' I can
   no longer
   hide
   I've gone the
   way of
   serpents
   an' can no
   longer find
   my way home

2. I need the
   wisdom of the
   ancients
   The sight of
   the soothsayers
   The salve of

the blues
A spiritual cathartic
or
I will strangle
in my own
filth
I will be but
a parody
of a woman
livin' a death
and life
that ends
with me,
with an aversion
to pain
that only allows for
a shallow
mediocrity; not
havin' the courage
to move past
old hurts I
remain bound in a
Peter Pan pubescence
And I am at once lost
and found unsure
of what is mine,
what is creation or
imitation, forward or
backward.
I have lost sight
of the Blk. Will
the seventies be
the times of
the Blind
Gropin' lost where is the vision?
All I see is the
crackers wasteland
a toilet left
unflushed
Malcom! And I'm a thousand years
behind the times
Nothin' has changed
ten years ago today I was
trickin' in L.A. now

I'm in New York and
I repeat nothin'
has changed!
I can't find my dreams
I don't know what
nothin' means.
I am alone. So ashamed
I keep going but
want to come
home.

3. Across the aisle from
me on the subway
a nigger in pink
jeans reads Ebony
magazine his
hair pressed and
curled
Elijah why did u leave us!
All I think of is gigs
costumes, gettin' slim, tryin' to MAKE
IT actin', dancin', maybe a play
on Broadway like Zaki
All the while the race
among the races is
at a crucial point
the survival of my people
is at stake
and I have elected
to spend my days
in petty pursuit
of pieces of the
pie. The shit
pie. I
am sick. I don't know
what it will take
to get me
well. Malcom is not goin' to rise
again. Panthers played out. Elijah is dead.
Processes is back. I can't talk about nobodi cause
I wear wigs. I can't write warrior poems talkin'
clean up the community cause I would
have to wash myself

away. I am a
part of the
perversion that
permeates our
existence
Blk children can
pass by taverns
and see me
on a platform
g-stringed and gyratin', hear me
cursin' on subways
and street corners
see me wid wite boys
and women. I repeat
I am sick
and do not know
what to do about
it. I have
come from the sixties to the
seventies. From being
the solution to
being the
problem.
They should stone me/US
I did not get this way ALONE.
I am a product of
humiliations, drowned dreams
and betrayals. It is
not all the time what
it seems. I tried/
tryin' and am still
gettin' up
I know in the end
it will be better
than it was an'
cannot berate myself
cause of limited
survival mechanisms
I am gettin' up
and gettin' on
Comin' home!
and don't
want no static
bout where

I been. I'm
comin' HOME an'
like the bible say
"let he who is
without sin
cast the first
stone"
I got to move past old ways
sometimes I jus' don't know how–
–I could be doin' better
but I could be doin'
worse
I have heard of those
who walk the way
of the new world. I don't
know how I came to always
be on the outside
lookin' in. Enlightened
ones do not leaves us. Oh robe
wearin'/Blk talkin'/knowledgeable
ones love us be
like my grandmother
whose prayers has
endured past all things
when the dancers stopped dancin'
poets stopped poetin'
men stopped lovin', her
prayers endured I
remember her
when ideologies
Kings and other things had
let me down and if
you can be like she
and never turn
your back on
your children
She said "go grow but don't
forget you can/must always
come home"

4. I have much
good to give
But don't feel

I have long
to live

5. changes pain

6. On the subway
home
people look at u
like u crazy
Blackmutherfuckers!
I was with a trick
last nite
Oh god! ain't no use
me talkin' about
it cause u can't know less
u been there. This nauseating
monkey/his hands with the nubs
factories had left him for fingers/cadillac/whiskey
drinkin' talkin' bout is it good?/u got
good pussy girl/tight stuff/ lemme rub it/lemme suck it good for u/
lemme grab some of dat tittie/
lemme rub—I'm not gonna put it back in—come on now
I'm gonna give u two twenty dollar bills/Do u suck?/
Aw honey u sumptin' else/I sho likes u/yo skin smooth as butter/
come to daddy lemme suck dat tittie

It was makin' me wanna die vomit
but the rent/tokens/dance classes/food/taxis/clothes
telephone/gas/lites/books/food/rent/entertainment
made me bite my lip an' say

Oh baby/it feels so good/Ahhh/Oh yeah honey
do it daddy

7. I feel empty
unfinished like
this poem
which has
no appropriate
end.

1977

Robin Becker

The Landing

1.
Intimate after weeks of close quarters,
warnings of scurvy, beer running low,
they watched the land mass
grow like another ocean
into sand cliffs one hundred feet high.

That morning, no tavern, no public house
received the ship; etched on a
piece of whalebone, it rocked;
scrimshaw designs of shrouds and stays
thrown into calmer waters.

Five year old Resolved White gave his hand
to his mother and followed her out of the hold.
Oceanus Brewster, born aboard ship,
had not even opened his eyes, when his father
scanned the shore, blinking back mountains
of twilled cotton and flax.

Leyden had made cloth merchants of them;
a handful of English, ill-at-ease
in the lowlands of Holland, turned
adventurers, soldiers of the Kingdom
of Christ, with a Church to found,
contracts to draw.

2.
From the shoaling
waters, pebbles
foam with the breakers,
slosh and splinter
over the sandbars
to the foreshore.

If you follow
one grain as it
oscillates

in the swash,
focus on the
small matter
of a single
reversal,
you will lose
the grain.

Somewhere, in the back-
wash, in a moment
of tumult, it
returns, over
the bars and
back, over the
bars and back.

3.

Dorothy Bradford waited for her husband.
Twice he had waved goodbye; twice
he had returned in the tiny shallop;
he brought tales of adventure at sea, and
once, someone else's harvest, several sacks of corn.

Six weeks anchored in Provincetown,
she stared at the coast and waited.
Bands of men sailed off to beach on the bars.
Each week brought them closer to winter.

Sealed into the sands of Provincetown's dunes
was her complaint; that a small child was left behind.
William had insisted. Too good to protest,
too Christian to argue,
she helped the other women with their children,
while the smell of fish—dead, fresh, decaying—
settled in her nostrils.

4.

They dug at the small mound, pushing
the sand back, like dogs,
to uncover a bone. Bowls, trays, beads,
a knife, the parcels the dead take

into the ground, they drew and
stuffed into satchels.

They did not uncover
the bones of a sea-fowl,
but the head and limbs of an Indian child
wrapped in string and bracelets.

5. Dorothy Bradford's Dream

The forest cover gives way; pitch pines
tumble down the soft shoulders, and beach grass
blows like hair down the broad backs of the dunes.
Two million tons of flashflooding sand
race into the harbor, seal the ship.
I am etched in a bed while the sand advances,
a bit of sleeve on a masthead,
falling fast.

6.

Sometime during the third expedition,
Dorothy prayed and slipped into the water.
When her husband, who would become
the first Governor, returned,
the shipmates tried to explain it.
It was an accident. They were so sorry.
She slipped. No one knew.
And no one knew.

1974

M.F. Hershman

Making Love to Alice

I imagine Gertrude making love to Alice
her generous and wise mouth upon her
breast her arms around hers the two
bodies fitting together, strangely
they are different and wonderfully they are
together. Gertrude being warm and full and
with Alice and Alice being warm and full with
Gertrude who is with her and the way
she is with her. Laughing. I imagine
they must know each other, the two, the one.

It is as with you and I. It is
with us as them. She then she and you then I
imagine. And in the act of imagining
make love to love to love to love

1976

Wendy Brooks Wieber

One, The Other, And

One

That sound like the scratch
scratch of an old recording
the static and scratch of an
old recording that tight
scratch was the sound of her
hands in her head and that
contracted scratch was the
scar of her mouth and her
eyes

That was she standing like
a phone booth at the corner;
folding door that groaned
and doubled at a man straddling
the rusty seat, facing a limp
phone, dialing a number's
name. A number and name
scratched on the wall of her
booth. A girl's name
scratched in an obscene erect
heart

And she began to think she
was that name, that girl. She
took her phone off the hook
and let the air wheeze out
the nozzle of her heart. Hid
her nickels and dimes. She took
time and more time to smile
the stitches of her mouth
and without bothering to file
her nails she folded
her hands in her
head

The Other

She made no sound
but held her body as
a driveling wind
held her own body in
and rocked it like a
painted rocking horse
she rocked like a huge
autistic child she rocked
a peeling circus pony
rocked with a bit
in her mouth painted
shut

She sat in the circus
and stood by the gorge.
Stood like a side show
hung in a wail
of the carnival wheel;
the jester laughing
blue bells on his toes
rapier in one blue glove.
Woman wearing a golden
mask and the lie
of one red plume.
Woman without nose.
Jester with curling toes.
Masquerade cursed
and carnival time.
The fault and a
face noosed by
darkness

And she thought she'd
noose the circus wheel and
waited to slash the glove
and all she had to do
was find the woman's
unborn nose, stamp the
jester's ringing toes.
But she waited by the chasm
holding body like a chill

fastening still ribs of pain,
biting noose in a mouth painted
shut. Playing with bright
blue carnival pills to rock
to rock to rock her slowly
stop

And

they hadn't known
of the gardens
the opalescent gardens
that swayed
behind their eyes
as tenuously as dew

that grew delicate leaves
shyly as the doe's eyes

They hadn't known
for so much frost
for bone cold fingers
of the stunting hand
and stings of the
ice bee

they hadn't known
but gathered themselves
unto one another
gathered their selves
into such a wholeness
they took
the blue knife
and slit the belly of night
spinning the sun into life

hands
stirring to opening
unwove the noose
and the sound of the scratch
and the scars
dissolved in the warming

of breaths
loosened like music

They hadn't known
that lovers touch
for love
not for province
that water intermingles
boundlessly with
water

And
the gardens unfolded
slendering
in sundance

the lovers
lay at one
another's breasts
and their hair
joined
like swiftly running
rivers
the dark murmur
and splashed gems
of deepest waters
while from their
very eyes
the garden

the greenest
singing leaves

grew
tendresses
of trust

1970

Eleanor Lerman

The Community of Women Causes an Operation

If you understood how much I need this
operation you would remove that revolver
from your hair and shoot your way out of
the women's museum
That's the story of my life doctor
the good girls I meet always show up wearing expensive
undergarments and John F. Kennedy Memorial Necklaces
You know, Jack, I used to be a woman until
I began suspecting these wet places on my body
of not remembering who they belong to
They can't simply belong to the community of women
If only someone could get me to a clinic
all the druggist does is rattle around in his bottles
and prescribe John F. Kennedy Memorial Vitamins
my god mr. president what's happened that we've both
come to this

1972

Finally I See Your Skin

Finally I see your skin so scarred
by my use that I can close my eyes and tell you
where the constant embrace of my fingers is turned to gold
on your stomach, and the press of my legs
has turned your thighs to polished glass
No one else thinks of touching you now
Your body mentions me in all its movements
and has come to fit only into my hands

I once told you that I had celestial information
cut on the insides of my mouth and it was years
before you wore it smooth enough to keep from
bleeding your tongue
Mindful of this
you come to kiss me one morning and find
I am old and brittle and pure
my mouth cracks open and planets start to pour out
universes form and begin to show
signs of life

1972

Jane Creighton

Ceres in an Open Field

If I would have a daughter
I would want her alone
for the first
long years together

I would want to write
her down exactly
I would want to talk
and touch and leave her

take her outside
the greenish fields
that quietly hold us
to ourselves. Smell her

I would want to smell her
chase her through steep canyons
to the watery desert
to the mouth of the water

she would leave me
spilling over the side
of a fabulous red
brick building into her body

she would scrape her knees
against the brick building
her bloody new knees
I would listen to her

healthy   screaming
I would record the bright colors
from her mouth
and make the picture

by which to know her
when I would see her again

1974

Rebecca Gordon

When I Was a Fat Woman

My silverware it seemed
was yoked to people's faces
always I'd lift a fork
and someone's eyebrow with it.

If I sat I settled
careful
to let the fat divide,
spill evenly
around the chair,
hug the stool the same
on either side.

If I ran I knew
behind me my hips
mocked every step
rocking
in parody
the fat rolling in
rolling out,
an evil tide

and snide in
what it said about me:
She eats, she eats
she puts it deep
in her mouth, she
sleeps dreaming of chocolate,
teeth churning the tasteless air,
she cares absurdly how
her salad's dressed
she saves the best
for last.

Waiters always winked at me
obscene in their complicity.
I'd yield

my passion

everywhere revealed;
every stranger knew
what I consented to
in private,

but oh in private!
The rough kiss of the biscuit,
the sour apple's scent
caressed me
asking nothing, asking only
to be known, to be devoured.
Oh my lovers, my enemies,
my sweet excess.

1978

Kitty Tsui

the words of a woman who breathes fire: one

yesterday,
had lunch with my Grandmother.
did her errands:
paid the phone bill, utilities,
mai leung juen dofu,
washed n waxed the floor,
me grumbling all the while, n
she grumbling all the while,
talkin bout
nee dow ah, there's dust here.
nee dow ah. m'hoo guum lahn ah.
aiyah, ngay jen leah feah,
chien sai loh.
washed n waxed the floor
on my hands n knees.

today had
leftover *dung gwa tong*
for breakfast,
cups of coffee n
apple pie for lunch.
wrote two poems, n
a letter to my sister
in college
at long beach.

I have stopped eating meat n
drinking alcohol.
when my mind is foggy
my dreams disintegrate
before I can grasp them.

I am a woman who speaks in silence.
I am into prayer
n other simple things.

I am not afraid of
talking back to those who
presume to know

who I am
n telling me that
what I do
is not natural.

I am afraid only
of forgetting
the Chinese Exclusion Act of 1882,

I am afraid only
of forgetting
Executive Order 9066/ Tule Lake,

I am afraid
only of
forgetting
the ancient wisdom of leaf
n soil n season.

1978

mai leung juen dofu (Chinese)—bought two pieces of dofu.
nee dow ah—here.
m'hoo guum lahn ah—don't be so lazy.
aiyah, ngay jen leah feah—you are very careless.
chien sai loh—you are a hopeless case.
dung gwa tong—wintermelon soup.
The Chinese Exclusion Act of 1882—one of the many anti-Chinese laws passed during the period 1868-1952 for the purpose of exclusion or taxation. This particular act banned the entrance of Chinese laborers, both skilled and unskilled, for ten years. The Geary Act of 1892 extended the 1882 Act for another ten years. In 1904 the Exclusion Acts were extended indefinitely.
Executive Order 9066—issued by Franklin Delano Roosevelt on February 19, 1942, sent 70,000 American citizens and 40,000 resident aliens of Japanese blood to wartime "relocation" camps. The Japanese were moved on notice as short as 48 hours in some cases, and allowed to take with them only as much baggage as they could carry. The camps were hastily constructed barracks or horse stalls, in desert or other sparsely populated areas, ringed with barbed wire and with armed military sentinels stationed in towers. *Tule Lake*, California (maximum population 18,789) was one of the World War II concentration camps, and one of the three camps where inmates revolted, led strikes and refused to cooperate.

—*K. T.*

Cherríe Moraga

Like I Am to No One

1.
I am your mother.
I want to get there in case you fall.
You could bleed to death on those rocks
if no one saw you.

I am your mother.
I watch you pull and flex
along the rocks, the deep dead drops
your loose bloused belly scraping
the jagged edges.

I am your mother.
I want to scale the side
of the cliff for you
retrieve you from these waters
if the situation
demands.

2.
We sleep in meadows together
mother and child. I stroke
the growth of your long limbs
huge back. I work and shape
your breasts & cunt into fuller
bodies—broadening, widening, pulling
stretching them out—watching
the armies of women
that pour
out of you.

Young fighters, marathon runners
paraders. They crawl out
single file onto the pool
of your stomach to swim
naked in it. Joining hands
they dance along the rim of your navel
to celebrate you, *their* mother.

I am your mother, I must warn you.
They will work their way into
the different parts of you. Some
will thrash into the wilds
of your arm pits to become jungle women.
Others will ride on the wave
of your ankles. Some will move
right into the backs of your earlobes
and whisper to you, prompting you
egging you on. You may go
dizzy from their persistent chanting.
Want to shake the devils
from your head.
Fear that they will work
their way into your scalp
and finally, your brain
where there will be no ridding
yourself of them.
But remember from where they came.

3.
We sleep naked on rocks together
mother and child, like flat
brown cakes baking, we sleep
pancaking eachother.

You want me to put my face into your breast.
You coax my stiffneck, bullhead there.
First, cheek to nipple
then lip
then my open mouth.

I weep
down the side
of the rock, relieved
of my motherhood.

1976

You Upset the Whole System of This Place

I've been inside all day.

you enter sleek, wet from winter rain. hot heaving chest.
hot breath. the still heatered air of this house melts
around your shoulders as you pass through it, dripping
down along your thighs to bare calloused feet. you
upset the whole system of this place.

approaching, your footsteps are solid and silent.

I, wrapped in bedclothes, billows of quilts and pillows.
I rock to the rhythmic sound of my own breathing inside
my head. stuffed mucus. my small chest, a battleground.
it is fragile and bony. a cough that scrapes it dry
each time. an ache like a rash beneath my ribs.

all that keeps you from me is this guatemalan drape
which lines my bed like mosquito net, only one simple
striped panel. you wave it aside with a backhand motion.
you move into the bed with me, not afraid of catching
cold. the thick warm dough of your hands pours into
the hollow parts of me.

> "I've been trying not to cry
> for you all day," I say.

you stroke my mouth closed.

> "I need you now. I have
> this terrible cold."

without reply, you go into the green kitchen and pull
out the remains of a gallon of cider. I imagine you
crushing the nutmeg into the liquid while it warms
over the low flame. squeezing in lemon, imitating me.

you return, mug in hand. you are dry now. your hair
straggly I drink the hot cider and you stay and roll
with me until dinnertime. you ease me a half an hour
into the night.

"Are you coming back?"
"Yes," you answer. "When you're better."
then I lean into your cheek, breathing in with my mouth.

I follow your footsteps exiting through the hardwood
hallway, down a step, across the carpet, out the door,
and down the many red wet steps into the night that
swallows you up.

1977

For the Color of My Mother

I am a white girl gone brown to the blood color of my mother
speaking for her through the unnamed part of the mouth
the wide-arched muzzle of brown women

at two
my upper lip split open
clear to the tip of my nose
it spilled forth a cry that would not yield
that travelled down six floors of hospital
where doctors wound me into white bandages
only the screaming mouth exposed

the gash sewn back into a snarl
would last for years

I am a white girl gone brown to the blood color of my mother
speaking for her

at five, her mouth
pressed into a seam
a fine blue child's line drawn across her face
her mouth, pressed into mouthing english
mouthing yes yes yes
mouthing stoop lift carry
(sweating wet sighs into the field
her red bandana comes loose from under the huge brimmed hat
moving across her upper lip)

at fourteen, her mouth
painted, the ends drawn up
the mole in the corner colored in darker larger mouthing yes
she praying no no no
lips pursed and moving

at forty-five, her mouth
bleeding into her stomach
the hole gaping growing redder
deepening with my father's pallor
finally stitched shut from hip to breastbone
        an inverted V
        Vera
        Elvira

I am a white girl gone brown to the blood color of my mother
speaking for her

as it should be
dark women come to me
                                        sitting in circles
I pass through their hands
the head of my mother
painted in clay colors

touching each carved feature
                                        swollen eyes and mouth
they understand the explosion the splitting
open   contained within the fixed expression

they cradle her silence
                                        nodding to me

1978

For Amber

when her friend Yve died of a stroke

I want to catch it while it's still fresh
and living in you, this talking like
you don't know what's gonna come out of your mouth
next. I watch the bodies pour
right out between those red lips of yours
and without thinking, they're changing
me—without trying, they're transforming
before my eyes.

I told you once
that you were like my grandmother
the white one, the gypsy
all dolled up
a white cadillac convertible
with Big Fins—she red deep
behind the wheel, her bleached blonde
flying. At stop lights she'd be there
just waiting for some sucker
to pull up, thinking she was
a gal of twenty. She'd turn
and flash him a seventy-year-old
smile, and press pedal.

Oh honey, this is you
in all your freeway glory,
the glamour of your ways.

And without stopping
last night you talked about the places
in you *thinking of your body*
that are lost to you, how we locate
the damage in our different parts
like a dead foot you said, how we run
inventory—checking on which show
promise of revival
and which don't.

What I didn't tell you
was how my grandmother
stopped all of a sudden

turned baby all of a sudden
speechless—
my momma giving her baths
in the tub, while I played,
her bare white skin slipping
down off those cold shoulders
piling up around her hips and knees,
slowing her down.

My grandma turned baby
and by the toilet I'd sit with her
she picking out designs in the linoleum,
saying this one looks like a man in a tub
scrubbing his back with a brush,
and it did.

1979

Barbara Noda

Strawberries

Father, your strawberry-stained
skin a field brown
as dark as your curses
of Mexicans
your hair now a
dusty legend
of the wavy-haired crow
who rode your forehead
for a lifetime,
you do not escape.

Sweet as lips puckered
to kiss
rows and rows of berries
there is nothing to say
when a man of
bad ancestry
inhales the fertile soil
plows his whole family
under and bitter and sodden
until one crop grows
and springs to life
an obsession.

Blood that is richer
than your blood
an inedible fruit
weaned on the sweat
of the son of a bitch
you and your 12-hour day
you do not escape
the strawberries
a dusk encrusted
shimmering
for a moment
plowed and plowed
a carcass/ a lifetime.

1976

Wendy Stevens

The Hymns My Mother Sang

hymns to the tunes
that
wove their way
through my ears and
childhood

that sat with me
in my closet
like haunting movies
too scared to go down
the hall alone
i sat
deciding if
it was her
still singing

away in the distance
blended on the
soft violet walls
near my sleep
they hung on the ruffles
of my bedspread
and formed a moat
around my dreams
visiting me
on small ships of
salt

floating down my face
caught on my tongue
nested deep inside of me
are the hymns my
mother sang

1973

Donna Allegra

A Rape Poem for Men

1.

Hey there brother man
Black prince come to save me from the white night
this piece is for you
just as much as it is for the each and every
sister in the room
who's been through the common
woman's experience of rape.
Yes my dark protector,
king, nation builder
I know you know about it
I can tell by your outrage about
white men
forcing Black women
white men
violating your sisters and queens
You know the hatred and ugliness
white men
can reap and sow on a field of women
how white men
can take their ugliness
and dump their garbage
and wipe themselves
on a woman
and then go to the boys around the corner
with a good joke on this dumb broad,
this silly bitch, this cunt
who told him no lies
who was maybe day dreaming
or just smiled
because it's no big deal
or because women weren't brought up to be rude
and it's a nice day—

why frown on it?
he smiled too
a nice-looking young man
features lovely like those sculptures
those African masks

a nice-looking bro
a face testifying to our people's beauty
our family's moral fiber
hell: not every dude out there
is asking for a nickel or some attention
some way not to look at himself
some hole to hide in.

2.

Being full grown means letting go of small comforts
means turning loose the short-term reliefs
that used to tide you over
until the next wad is shot
and your personal load of sticky stuff
is dropped into someone else's lap,
is made her trial by fire
just because you can't bear to face yourself
You can be lost on high with the vision
of some woman under a gun
on her knees to you,
but understand this:
in time the temporary reliefs
reach the point of diminishing returns
and the bitch will turn around
with a big hungry mouth calling for payback
On this Saturday night double-bill
is your self-respect,
your two feet,
your right to stand and walk tall,
all those things you can never own
You'll be the one fucked between your legs,
in your mouth,
up your ass,
all in your head,
every place you can be fucked
and then try to find yourself left alone
and bleeding and violated and furious
beyond reach or reason
crying after something you lost
because you were playing and abusing yourself
spilling rotten wine and sowing shit
You'll see real clear
them two balls and your dick

that now you'll handle with care
because some once polite lady
is going to turn her head away
and you'll pull the trigger
to shoot yourself off
wham, bam, just like a man.

1976-1980

When People Ask

for Cenen and Sayeeda who gave it to me

When people ask who you are
say you are Africa
say that the strange tangle of dread
is soft and clean-curling nappy hair,
that your nose wide and flared
breathes in fresh thoughts
and sniffs out good things to eat,
that your yellow brown black
blue purple skin
is a stunning rainbow pot of gold
a kettle simmering yams
calabash rattling music
drums kicking complex rhythms
the weave, a cloth for the dance
Say that deep into the night
a house of sisters sat up telling each other
their hopes and dreams
eased their young anxieties
giving of their experiences
passing on their knowledge of life,
that their love for all each other
was anchored in waves of differences
all showing the many ways of being,
that after rocking and sharing
and love and questions and laughter
and knowing that their love would be for always
the sun rose red to show them the boats
coming to gut your shore, Africa
Say that the house of sisters easy with love
went out to welcome

a people shades paler
than your warm humanity
who then ripped your seeds from root
and from one another
onto different boats where
others too, had been taken from your lap
to as many places as there were of them
and the crack of the whip held them there,
locked away from each other's love
that was meant to be for always
Africa, say that their spirit did not die
and after many, many years
each one separately got over
and found her own way to live
and after a time,
each one from the house of sisters
was drawn to a place
    one came riding
    one swam the waters
    one told others' stories
    one danced her life together
    one lifted a voice that thrilled the heavens
    one could speak in cloth
    one had hands for healing
Say that they found one another
and though not recognizing her very sister
but following the scent of memory
they all eventually came,
each one from the house of sisters
many nights together
telling each other their hopes and dreams
eased their young anxieties
giving of their experiences
passing on their knowledge of life,
that their love for all each other
was anchored in waves of differences
all showing the many ways of being,
that after rocking and sharing
and love and questions and laughter
and knowing that their love would be for always
the sun rose red, the memory spread all over the morning
and touched them to the root
as they looked around and knew
that this place was not their home, Africa

and it was then that a mighty ache
of anger frustration revelation promise came
sure as the love that was meant to be for always,
had brought them once more together
When people ask who you are
with your mane of dread sprouting fire
your nose so fierce, flaring
your bald faced beauty roaring–
you the dragon breathing the wind
upon your many-breasted warriors
say that you are Africa
and that a house of sisters has come
Say that you are Africa
who birthed the rainbow children
and that they who ask must also remember
the house of sisters
Africa–a spirit risen
not from the dead
but a life run underground
now swelling to the surface
in your children's dreams now awakened
Say that you are Africa come calling
Say it until the children of every house
can give the same answer
Say it so that there's never again
the question denying
Who you are
Say: You are Africa.

1980

Osa Hidalgo-de la Riva

She's

we stay awake until the wee hours of the night because we are free americanos. we can send women home. watch women out our window of third story victorian existence. call nineteen year old possibilities. drink tequila. dance. sing. cry. make mistakes. grow. die.

la semana de la raza. we cruise the streets with the rest of the cruising youth. she was not used to one night stands even though we had already become a fourth or fifth. mamá y la familia mestiza calls.

the moon has refused to become full. my dream content of a play has moved away. las mujeres outside my window have taken down their puerto rican blue curtains.

mí tia sleeps under a heat controlled casa. she knows she has heard me if only for a second. la gente de la misión know that they have heard me being serious. seen me being for real. they know that they know that.

my mama needs a typewriter. she needs some income too. i am on my way to the giant earthquake with my smith corona. south where the land is quaking with my heart. why are women so goddamned scared of women. you know that you know that.

i have to fall asleep believing en la luna i slept under en méxico. the one that promised protection. if i cannot sleep, at least i will be able to understand.

i can fill up this whole white page because i write papers now with ease. i stay up all night spending raza time typing papers for white men until i get sick of all the gringoness.

it is then that i desire to borrow the morning bird's wings and follow the family of trees south. borrow somoza's gun and turn it against him under este quinto sol. paint his chest the color of the robin's.

1979

la semana de la raza (Spanish)— the week of the race (celebrated during the week of cinco de mayo, fifth of may).
mamá y la familia mestiza—mother and the family of mixed bloods.
las mujeres—the women.
mi tía—my aunt.
la gente de la misión—the people of the mission.
la luna—the moon.
en mexico—in méxico.
raza—race, lineage, family.
gringoness—condition or quality given to foreigners, especially english and north-americans.
este quinto sol—this fifth sun (according to mayan and aztec culture we are under the fifth sun).

—O.H.R.

Felice Newman

Sister

after Gabriela Mistral

There is a woman walks as I walk, carrying packages over her hip as we would carry children. Her boots cut deep holes in the snow, and I want to take her home.

In all of this town there is no water. Behind a curtain, there is a candle filling a bowl with wax. A field of women, each bent over her stoop, scraping deep furrows in the ice. My hands dig into her coat. We walk, and our legs are strong for work. If my breasts are hard and cold, then the winter has come inside me. I touch her scarf. Because we kneel at my door, in spring the yards will sink with so much wetness.

1978

Lesbian Poetry in the Classroom

Contributors' Biographies

Work by Contributors

Some Additional Resources

Lesbian Poetry in the Classroom

by Elly Bulkin

I.

Teaching women's poetry at all is, I think, nearly always a struggle: an effort to overcome most students' resistance to reading poetry by encouraging them to open to the personal immediacy, the urgency, the language and rhythm of contemporary women's poetry. Teaching lesbian poetry is even more difficult: non-lesbian teachers and students bring to it a multi-layered set of assumptions that must be dealt with before the poetry itself can be explored.

An unknown to most of us, lesbian poetry, like lesbianism, is understandably threatening. When we think about teaching lesbian poetry, what most of feel is fear. We hesitate to write about it in detail (if at all) for the same reasons that we hesitate to emphasize it—or even discuss it—in class and out. The fear of losing our jobs, of being denied tenure. The fear that, regardless of our sexual and affectional preference, we will be dismissed by our students as "just a lesbian." The concern that students who feel hostile or skeptical or even friendly toward feminism and the women's movement will be irretrievably "lost" if "too much" attention were directed toward the issue of lesbianism. The doubts about our colleagues' reactions to what we teach and how we teach it. The threat that the validity of a hard-earned women's course, women's studies program, or women's center will be undercut, and funding jeopardized, if it becomes perceived as a "dyke effort."[1]

The continued presence of this oppression is reflected in many ways. For all that has been written about teaching women's literature, detailed explorations of the impact on teachers and students of a discussion of lesbian literature (or anything else relating directly to lesbians) are conspicuously absent. From otherwise useful articles about classroom approaches and dynamics, we get little sense of ways to deal with lesbianism, let alone lesbian poetry. Each teacher does so, if at all, in a comparative vacuum, and hardly ever with space to dialogue with colleagues and/or friends about the issues that might be raised in the classroom.

Even for people who do acknowledge the existence of lesbian writers, the temptation to deny the significance of a writer's lesbianism is powerful in educational institutions that reflect society's general homophobia. About seven years ago, when I was teaching at an urban community college, I rather naively suggested a new course for the syllabus called "The

Outsider in Twentieth-Century American Literature," which was to deal with the writings of lesbians and gay men and of people who were or had been in prison or mental hospitals. When it was brought up at the English Department meeting (after enthusiastic approval by the appropriate committee), I was totally taken aback because everyone discussed it—with much laughter and side comments—as if I had suggested a course about homosexuality and literature.

Most of the faculty dismissed the course by saying, "Well, *that's* not so important. I don't see why that has any more influence on a writer than a thousand other things." No one was willing to consider the impact on one's writing of "having to live as a 'different' person in a heterosexist culture."[2] The course's chances for support disappeared under the weight of peer disparagement and discomfort. The feelings were so strong that a discussion of the academic "respectability"—or the true breadth—of the course content never took place.

My own failure at that point—and that of other lesbian and gay male faculty members—to speak out *as outsiders* aborted any further educating/radicalizing potential in the department meeting. Although not, of course, a classroom situation, the meeting reminds me of many classes in which I have since spoken as an open lesbian: the same personal discomfort; the same annoyance at having the issue raised at all; the same denial of the impact of lesbianism on literature; the same need of most women to go on record as being apart from lesbian women.

For any teacher who is not a lesbian, these responses need to be explored before she can effectively teach material dealing with lesbianism. The reactions of non-lesbian teachers and students to a poet's lesbianism stand, most often, as a significant barrier to her work. For the teacher, overcoming this barrier is especially important because of her general function as role model in the classroom. If she feels uncomfortable with the subject matter, but insists that she has "no difficulty at all" with lesbianism, she will teach the inappropriateness of discussing (and perhaps even recognizing) such discomfort. If she begins a class on lesbian poetry by "just happening" to mention her married status, she communicates her fear of being suspected a lesbian and discourages her students from asking "too many" questions or seeming "too interested."

If, on the other hand, she acknowledges the limitations of her own understanding of lesbianism and makes available information she has learned from lesbians or from a number of current books by lesbians, she will support her students' willingness to fill the gaps in their own knowledge. If she admits her own fears, her own stereotypes, her own myths, and places them within the framework of a society that has taught homophobia to each of us, and taught us well, she will help make the barrier to the poetry less formidable. She will also affirm the importance of taking risks in order better to understand the experiences and perceptions of women who differ significantly from herself and her non-lesbian students. At the 1977 Modern Language Association panel on lesbians and literature, Audre Lorde said:

> And where the words of women are crying to be heard, we must each of us recognize our responsibility to seek those words out, to read them and share them and examine them in their pertinence to our lives. That we not hide behind the mockeries of separation that have been imposed upon us and which so often we accept as our own: for instance, "I can't possibly teach black women's writings—their experience is so different from mine," yet how many years have you spent teaching Plato and Shakespeare and Proust? Or another: "She's a white woman and what could she possibly have to say to me?" Or "She's a lesbian, what would my husband say, or my chairman?" Or again, "This woman writes of her sons and I have no children." And all the other ways in which we rob ourselves and each other.[3]

Although I do think that a non-lesbian teacher should deal with lesbian poetry in any case, to raise the relevant personal and political issues and to explore them most adequately require facilitation by a lesbian teacher, a lesbian student, a lesbian guest speaker, by someone who has herself experienced the freedom and oppression of being a lesbian and who can share that openly.[4]

My own perspective on teaching lesbian material parallels in some ways that of the identifiably lesbian teacher: when I speak in a classroom about lesbian poetry, I do so as a lesbian. But, since I usually am a guest lecturer, I have the freedom to teach one or two sessions of a class without the regular lesbian teacher's very real concerns about both her economic and professional survival and her ongoing relationships with students, colleagues, and administrators. When teaching lesbian poetry, I begin with two fundamental assumptions: the poet's lesbianism is an essential, not an incidental, fact about her life and her work; and a discussion of lesbianism must focus not only on our political ideas (what we think), but on our feelings (how we act, what we say, how we live our expressed politics).

II.

Students in one women's studies class were adamant about the "universality" of the selections in *Amazon Poetry*. Why, they wanted to know, had Joan Larkin and I called it "an anthology of *lesbian* poetry" (my italics)? Skeptical about my answers, they held to their sense of ready identification with the poets in the book; the fact of the poets' lesbianism was not, they insisted, sufficiently important for us to have stressed it. Other questions followed, more personal ones. I responded to their questions about coming out, being a lesbian mother, my parents' reactions to my lesbianism, lesbian sexuality, the relationship between lesbianism and feminism. I shared my feelings about the energy and time it took me even to be in the class, to answer all of those questions; I recalled times when my anger at the need to deal with people's homophobia and general ignorance about lesbianism had been too strong for me to be able to do so.

Although I have almost never been the only lesbian in such a class, I run the risk (unless other lesbians are vocal) of having my own perceptions and experiences applied to lesbians as a group. I emphasized that I was speaking as an individual. A white, middle class, able-bodied, comparatively young woman, I stressed my obvious inability to speak for the many lesbians who are American Indian, Asian-American, Black, Latin, poor or working class, disabled, older.

After I began a second meeting of the same class with a twenty-minute reading from *Amazon Poetry*, we moved to a deeper level of dialogue. Most of the students had managed to "forget" Audre Lorde's "Love Poem"; others had felt too uncomfortable at its explicitness to initiate a discussion about it:

And I knew when I entered her I was
high wind in her forests hollow
fingers whispering sound
honey flowed
from the split cups
impaled on a lance of tongues
on the tips of her breast on her navel
and my breath
howling into her entrances
through lungs of pain.

My reading seemed to give students "permission" to relate to and share their fears and confusion. Our point of departure was the visual image of two women loving each other physically. We spoke of the Western tradition of love poetry with its nearly total preoccupation—when sexually explicit—with intercourse. One woman said that because she was just starting to explore her own sexuality, references to anything sexual embarrassed her. Another said that because she couldn't identify with either woman in the poem, she had great difficulty relating to it.

Finally we began to discuss what makes lesbianism so threatening. A woman remembered a disparaging, upsetting comment made the day before by a male friend who had seen her with *Amazon Poetry* in the college library. A second commented that she found it hard to overcome her resistance to thinking about lesbianism, her feeling that I shouldn't be "bothering" her about it.

We spoke of the homophobia in the denial of our own and others' lesbianism. We looked at Susan Sherman's "Lilith of the Wildwood, of the Fair Places":

> women   women surround me
> images of women   their faces
> I   who for years   pretended them away
> pretended away their names   their faces
> myself   what I am   pretended it away

I spoke of the form of denial in Sherman's early love poetry: her use of the ambiguous pronoun "you" and the absence of specifically female sexual imagery; instead, in the early and late sixties, she described her subject subtly, through gentle images of grass, of rain, of "how the earth opens its body Almost/as an act of grace."[5] Reviewing *With Anger/With Love* several years ago, I had been pleased to conclude accurately from such images that Sherman was a lesbian poet (although I printed the review only after having had this confirmed); I had been appropriately embarrassed in 1973 (after I had come out as a lesbian) to find out that I had assumed mistakenly that the "you" in a love poem by Lorraine Sutton was a man.[6]

We discussed other forms of denial. I had needed to be *told*, for example, in 1971 by a friend of eleven years' standing that she and the woman she lived with were lovers, that they did *not* use their second bedroom for anything but guests. I connected my own past liberalism on sexual/affectional matters ("Anything people want to do is OK with me as long as it doesn't hurt anyone.") with the ready acceptance of lesbianism that had been verbalized during the first class meeting by women who were now admitting to much more complex feelings. By now, the limitations of such "liberalism" seemed clear. I connected it to a tendency to see selectively, to homogenize, to focus on women's shared experiences to the exclusion of those profoundly influenced by sexual and affectional preference, as well as by other significant differences among us.

I stressed that the experiences of lesbian and non-lesbian women *are* different. Blurring the distinctions only denies the realities of many women's lives. Understanding that is a way into ourselves and into the poetry. I read aloud the final section of Olga Broumas' "Sleeping Beauty":

> City-center, mid-
> traffic, I

wake to your public kiss. Your name
is Judith, your kiss a sign

to the shocked pedestrians, gathered
beneath the light that means
stop
in our culture
where red is a warning, and men
threaten each other with final violence: *I will drink*
your blood. Your kiss
is for them

a sign of betrayal, your red
lips suspect, unspeakable
liberties as
we cross the street kissing
against the light, singing, *This*
is the woman I woke from sleep, the woman that woke
me sleeping.

I wondered aloud whether someone who was not aware of the extent to which lesbian and non-lesbian women lead different lives can appreciate fully the impact of these lines. It is the daily oppression, not the pink triangle and the Nazi concentration camps (in which up to a quarter million lesbians and gay men were executed): simply two women who cannot, without shock, disgust, possible physical violence from passersby, show affection on a city street.[7] "I am a pervert," Judy Grahn writes, "therefore I have learned/to keep my hands to myself in public."

I linked my own experiences, my own anger with that of the poets. I do not want my own reality to be distorted by someone's insistence that my life is "just like" that of a heterosexual woman. We ended the class with my reading Adrienne Rich's words:

> Two friends of mine, both artists, wrote me about reading the *Twenty-One Love Poems* with their male lovers, assuring me how "universal" the poems were. I found myself angered, and when I asked myself why, I realized that it was anger at having my work essentially assimilated and stripped of its meaning, "integrated" into heterosexual romance. That kind of "acceptance" of the book seems to me a refusal of its deepest implications. The longing to simplify, to defuse feminism by invoking "androgyny" or "human-

ism," to assimilate lesbian experience by saying that "relationship" is really all the same, love is always difficult—I see that as a denial, a kind of resistance, a refusal to read and hear what I've actually written, to acknowledge what I am.[8]

III.

As teachers, we make choices which, consciously or not, reflect such denial. I wonder, for example, how many women's studies teachers are using as texts Rich's *Diving into the Wreck* (1973), *Poems: Selected and New, 1950-1974* (1975), or the Norton Critical Edition, *Adrienne Rich's Poetry* (1975). Do they choose to teach poems from these earlier books to the exclusion of the more recent, explicitly lesbian poetry in *The Dream of a Common Language* (1978)? How prepared are they to explore this change with students who probably believe, among other myths, that they can always identify a lesbian, that women "discover" their lesbianism at an early age, that their own heterosexual lifestyles are comfortably fixed? How do they feel about the poetry of this fifty-one-year-old woman who raised three sons, this lesbian who writes, "I choose to walk here. And to draw this circle"?

As teachers, they can choose to ignore a poem like Rich's "For Judith, Taking Leave," written in 1962, but not published until *Poems: Selected and New, 1950-1974*:

> . . . that two women
> in love to the nerves' limit
> with two men—
> shared out in pieces
> to men, children, memories
> so different and so draining—
> should think it possible
> now for the first time
> perhaps, to love each other
> neither as fellow-victims
> nor as a temporary
> shadow of something better . . . .
>
> that two women can meet
> no longer as cramped sharers
> of a bitter mutual secret
> but as two eyes in one brow

receiving at one moment
the rainbow of the world.

Speaking in a 1976 interview about her decision to withhold this poem from publication for so long, Rich said:

> When I wrote that, I didn't think of it as a lesbian poem. This is what I have to keep reminding myself—that at that time I did not recognize, I did not name the intensity of those feelings as I would name them today, *we* did not name them. When I first chose not to publish that poem, I thought, this is just a very personal poem, an occasional poem, it doesn't carry the same weight or interest as other poems I would publish. But my dismissing of it was akin to my dismissing of the relationship, although in some ways I did not dismiss it—it was very much with me for a long time.[9]

Looking at Rich's poetry today with the knowledge of her lesbianism and then "dismissing" that knowledge as "less than essential" to the teaching of her poetry, without sufficient "weight or interest," perhaps too risky for students, colleagues, administrators, is to censor a vital part of contemporary women's poetry:

Homesick for myself, for her—as, after the heatwave
breaks, the clear tones of the world
manifest: cloud, bough, wall, insect, the very soul of light
homesick as the fluted vault of desire
articulates itself: *I am the lover and the loved,*
home and wanderer, she who splits
firewood and she who knocks, a stranger
in the storm, two women, eye to eye
measuring each other's spirit, each other's
limitless desire,
a whole new poetry beginning here.

Although a teacher can choose to teach Rich's poetry without totally upsetting the academic concept of what constitutes "good" poetry, the decision to teach a poet like Judy Grahn is immediately more complicated. Working-class, female, and lesbian, Grahn has never had a stake in the established literary tradition and its social/political/aesthetic values. She seems, at times, to mock them intentionally: she calls one book *Edward the Dyke and Other Poems*, even though the title work is clearly in prose and the word "dyke" can hardly help the book slip unobtrusively onto a college reading list.

First published in what now seems another era, one offering comparatively little lesbian poetry, her poems have helped to establish a tradition of women's/lesbian poetry that is personal, accessible, non-hierarchical. One rhythmic and ironic eight-line poem makes us look again at everyday language:

> I am the wall at the lip of the water
> I am the rock that refused to be battered
> I am the dyke in the matter, the other
> I am the wall with a womanly swagger
> I am the dragon, the dangerous dagger
> I am the bulldyke, the bulldagger
>
> and I have been many a wicked grandmother
> and I shall be many a wicked daughter.

Most often, she seems to hide the "craft" of her poems, giving the impression that she wrote them quickly—without careful attention to structure and language and rhythm.

In "A Woman Is Talking to Death," a deceptively "non-poetic" opening, the narrative of a motorcyclist killed instantaneously on a bridge, leads into a tightly woven series of events, prose interrogations, lyric passages, and recurrent phrases that create a painfully wonderful poem that has become something of a touchstone of lesbian-feminist writing. "That's a fact," Grahn keeps observing as she builds image after image of women ignored, derided, abused. The central "fact" of the poem is finally the poet's own lesbianism. In a society that perceives lesbians as committing "indecent acts" and that leers at women who kiss each other, who call each other "lovers," who admit to "wanting" another woman, Grahn forces a rethinking of both language and the assumptions behind it. In "a mock interrogation," the fourth section of this nine-part poem, Grahn writes:

> . . . I confess to kissing the top of a 55 year old woman's head in the snow in boston, who was hurt more deeply than I have ever been hurt, and I wanted her as very few people have wanted me—I wanted her and me to own and control the city we lived in, to staff the hospital I knew would mistreat her, to patrol the streets controlling the men who would murder or disfigure or disrupt us, not accidentally with machines, but on purpose, because we are not allowed out on the street alone—
>
> Have you ever committed any indecent acts with women?

> Yes, many. I am guilty of allowing suicidal women to die before my eyes or in my ears or under my hands because I thought I could do nothing. I am guilty of leaving a prostitute who held a knife to my friend's throat to keep us from leaving, because we would not sleep with her, we thought she was old and fat and ugly; I am guilty of not loving her who needed me; I regret all the women I have not slept with or comforted, who pulled themselves away from me for lack of something I had not the courage to fight for, for us, our life, our planet, our city, our meat and potatoes, our love. These are indecent acts, lacking courage, lacking a certain fire behind the eyes, which is the symbol, the raised fist, the sharing of resources, the resistance that tells death he will starve for lack of the fat of us, our extra. Yes I have committed acts of indecency with women and most of them were acts of omission. I regret them bitterly.

In classes where I have read aloud these lines, students have spoken of being moved by them, of reacting emotionally to the lesbian oppression Grahn describes. For students who do not themselves share that oppression, poetry that can transcend that gap in experience is, I think, especially important to teach. For students in women's studies or other courses who associate feminism and lesbianism exclusively with white, economically privileged women and of poetry as the province of the well-to-do and formally educated, Grahn's writing destroys more than one erroneous assumption.

Still more issues get raised when a teacher decides to teach the work of lesbian poets who suffer additional oppression because they are Asian-American, Black, Latina, or Native American, as well as of more than one racial/ethnic heritage. If homophobia throws up one formidable barrier between lesbian poetry and the non-lesbian reader, racism adds one that is at least as high for the non-Third World reader—and teacher—of poetry by lesbians of color. Those of us who are white teachers of this poetry need, I think, to be prepared to approach directly the issue(s) of racism, even as we recognize the complexity and difficulty of doing so.[10]

While most of the non-lesbian students I have taught have had strong negative responses to the explicit lesbian sexuality in Lorde's "Love Poem," most of the white students have had equally strong responses to her poem, "Power," about the acquittal of a white police officer in the fatal shooting of a ten-year-old Black boy:

> Today that 37 year old white man with 13 years of police forcing
> was set free
> by 11 white men who said they were satisfied
> justice had been done

and one black woman who said "They convinced me"
meaning
they had dragged her 4'10" black woman's frame
over the hot coals of four centuries of white male approval
until she let go the first real power she ever had
and lined her own womb with cement
to make a graveyard for our children.

I have not been able to touch the destruction within me.
But unless I learn to use the difference
between poetry and rhetoric
my power too will run corrupt as poisonous mold
or lie limp and useless as an unconnected wire
and one day I will take my teenaged plug
and connect it to the nearest socket
raping an 85 year old white woman who is somebody's mother
and as I beat her senseless and set a torch to her bed
a greek chorus will be singing in 3/4 time
"Poor thing. She never hurt a soul. What beasts they are."

Faced with white students who focused on the pain of the eighty-five-year-old white woman to the near or total exclusion of the dead boy, the Black woman on the jury, or the poet herself, I have talked about the need both to empathize with someone else's pain and to distinguish between institutional violence and violence that is a ("corrupt") response to it. Faced with students who argue that "anyone" could have written this poem, I have stressed the importance of reading it as a statement by someone who *is* Black, and therefore identifies strongly with a boy shot by a policeman who "said in his own defense 'I didn't notice the size or nothing else/ only the color' . . . ." Faced with white students who have found it difficult enough to read Lorde as "just" a political Black poet, and by Black non-lesbian students who clearly have preferred to focus exclusively on her Black identity, I have stressed that she is a lesbian, a mother, a feminist, a teacher, a poet who has also written:

I have no sister no mother no children
left
only a tideless ocean of moonlit women
in all shades of loving
learning the dance of electrical tenderness
no father no mother would teach them.[11]

Such poetry underscores once again the importance of not simplifying, not homogenizing, of recognizing fully the significant differences among individual lesbian poets, as well as the difference between poets who define themselves as lesbians and poets who do not. Although I would not argue that having all of this information about a given poet is always essential to a reading of her poetry, I do think that it often makes a crucial difference in how we choose to read and then teach a poet's work.

To teach such poems we need to model the kind of openness and directness in exploring lesbianism in the classroom that we would like our students to adopt. I recognize the difficulties of doing this—for women who define themselves as lesbians and for women who do not. Still, I do not believe that we can effect positive, radical changes in our students (and in ourselves) without pushing beyond feminist analysis and thought to an approach that combines these with the personal exploration which can lead to basic change.

IV.

Even as I put forth such an approach to teaching lesbian poetry, I am fully aware of the growing number of external obstacles to it. This past summer a University of Texas teacher "lost her teaching job because she invited speakers from Austin Lesbian/Gay Political Caucus and Austin Lambda to speak to her class on 'The Politics of American Culture'."[12] Oklahoma has already passed a law that closely paraphrases California's defeated Briggs initiative: "to fire or refuse to hire . . . any teacher, counselor, aide or administrator (in the public school system) . . . who advocates, solicits, encourages, or promotes private or public homosexual activity . . . that is likely to come to the attention of students or parents . . . ." The Oklahoma law prohibits *anyone* who assumes its essential validity from discussing lesbianism (or male homosexuality) in the classroom.[13] Although aimed specifically at public school teachers, such right-wing legislation seems designed to effect repression and witch hunts throughout the educational system. Along with the lesbian and gay rights ordinances being consistently rejected or repealed across the country, such legislation makes concrete institutionalized homophobia and further compounds the difficulties both of teaching lesbian poetry and of being—and being identified as—a lesbian.

The case for lesbian poetry can, of course, be allowed to rest on the academically acceptable belief in literary quality. Teaching it does, after all, expose students to much of the "best" of contemporary women's writing. But teaching it as *lesbian* poetry moves us to shakier, less traditionally academic ground. In its conscious risk-taking, in its affirmation of our diversity, exploring lesbianism and lesbian poetry as an integral part of women's lives and literature constitutes one facet of what the National Women's Studies Association has characterized as women's studies "at its best": "a vision of a world free not only from sexism but also from racism, class-bias, ageism, heterosexual bias–from all the ideologies and institutions that have consciously or unconsciously oppressed and exploited some for the advantage of others."[14] And such exploration adds one more, badly-needed voice to the struggle to achieve some semblance of justice and compassion in this country.

Notes

[1] Peg Cruikshank's experience reveals an important aspect of this problem: "I had been on campus less than a week when a woman professor said to me: 'Now, Peg, don't let those lesbians take over the women's center.' Curious, I went to the center to ask what it offered for lesbians. Nothing. 'We haven't been able to get any lesbians to come here,' said the person in charge. So much for lesbian takeover" (*Radical Teacher, 6* [December, 1977], 37). See also Bulkin's "Heterosexism and Women's Studies," *Radical Teacher* (December, 1980); Cruikshank's "Lesbians in Academia," in *Our Right to Love: A Lesbian Resource Book*, ed. Ginny Vida, produced in cooperation with the women of the National Gay Task Force (Englewood Cliffs, N.J.: Prentice-Hall, 1978), pp.164-166; and Judith McDaniel's "Is There Room for Me in the Closet or My Life as the Only Lesbian Professor," *Heresies No. 7*, Vol.2, No.3 (Spring, 1979), pp.36-39.

[2] Adrienne Rich in "An Interview with Adrienne Rich: Part I" by Elly Bulkin, *Conditions: One* (Spring, 1977), p.58.

[3] "The Transformation of Silence into Language and Action," *Sinister Wisdom, 6* (Summer, 1978), p.14; reprinted in Lorde's *The Cancer Journals* (Argyle, N.Y.: Spinsters, Ink, 1980), p.23.

[4] Teachers wanting a lesbian speaker but unaware of local groups that might be able to provide such a speaker can consult the "Lesbian National Resource List" in *Our Right to Love*, pp.288-318 or contact the Lesbian Herstory Archives, P.O. Box 1258, New York, N.Y. 10001.

[5] "Duration " *With Anger/With Love* (Amherst: Mulch Press, 1974), p.15.

[6] Bulkin, "Beyond the Word," *Majority Report* (August 8, 1974), p.10; "Poetry," *Majority Report* (January 11, 1975), p.9.

[7] Ira Glasser, "The Yellow Star and the Pink Triangle," *The New York Times*, September 10, 1977, Op Ed Page. Glasser's figure for the number of lesbians and gay men executed by the Nazis is for the period 1937-1945; they were required to wear pink triangles in the concentration camps.

[8] Adrienne Rich in "An Interview with Adrienne Rich: Part II," *Conditions: Two* (Fall, 1977), p.58.

[9] "An Interview with Adrienne Rich: Part I," p.64.

[10] Some of the basic issues involved are discussed in Margaret Strobel, "Fighting Two Colonialisms: Thoughts of a White Feminist Teaching about Third World Women," *Radical Teacher, 6* (December, 1977), pp.20-23; and Nancy Hoffman, "White Woman, Black Women: Inventing an Adequate Pedagogy," *Women's Studies Newsletter*, 5 (Spring, 1977), pp.21-24. Hoffman writes: "There are two principles for white women who would teach about black women. First, do your research and class preparation more thoroughly than you would for teaching about your own female tradition or the majority white male Anglo-American one. You must be able to gen-

eralize about black women's culture when appropriate, and you will probably feel ill at ease when doing so. Second, be prepared to play dual and conflicting roles; only sometimes will your own anti-racism and your solidarity with other women protect you from representing the group oppressing black women" (p.22). These comments are particularly relevant when the teacher of poetry by lesbians of color is both white *and* heterosexual. See also Bulkin, "Racism and Writing: Some Implications for White Lesbian Critics," *Sinister Wisdom 13* (Spring 1980), pp.3-22; Barbara Smith, "Racism and Women's Studies," *Frontiers* (Spring 1980), pp.48-49· Adrienne Rich, "Disloyal to Civilization: Feminism, Racism, Gynephobia," *On Lies, Secrets, and Silence: Selected Prose, 1966-1978* (New York: Norton, 1979), pp.275-310; and *Top Ranking: A Collection of Essays on Racism and Classism in the Lesbian Community*, ed. Sara Bennett and Joan Gibbs (Brooklyn: February 3rd Press, 1980), $3.50 from Bennett/Gibbs, 306 Lafayette Ave., Brooklyn, N.Y. 11238.

[11] "Scar," *The Black Unicorn* (New York: Norton, 1978), p.49.

[12] "No Gay Teaching," *off our backs* (December 1980), p.14.

[13] John Mehring, "The Briggs Initiative is Alive and Well—and Living in Oklahoma," *Gay Community News*, Vol.6, No.49 (July 7, 1979), pp.8-9; Jeanne Cordova, "Rights and Referendums," *Lesbian Tide*, 8 (July/August, 1978), p.14.

[14] "Constitution of the National Women's Studies Association," *Women's Studies Newsletter*, 5 (Spring, 1977), p.6.

Contributors' Biographies

Donna Allegra, *b. 1953, Brooklyn.* Born, survived several suspended animations, rose as androgyne parent to myself as tomboy butch Amazon turning over some soft edges. Will write forever: poetry, essays, fiction. Went steady with a journal at 14—I'm a lifer now. It takes my thoughts, feelings, observations on life and people. You can know me by my composition notebook.

Paula Gunn Allen, *b. 1939, Cubero, New Mexico.* Laguna/Sioux-Lebanese-American. My ancestry includes renegade Indians, Scots, Lebanese. On my mother's side my New Mexican roots go back some several thousand years, so you can say I'm a native. Raised in a multilingual (Laguna-English-Spanish-German-Arab) household, I speak/write mostly only English. My children are hippies (what choice did they have) and musicians—except the youngest who will be an artist. My writing, like my background, is totally atypical. I wouldn't know a main street if it came up and tapped me on the shoulder. But I do know the land—the high mesas, the endless rocks and dirt, the struggling plant life, the sky, the clouds, the sun, the stars.

Dorothy Allison, *b. 1949, South Carolina.* Dorothy Allison was born in Greenville to an enormous family that has since lost track of her. Primarily an anthropologist, she believes that as long as she avoids working waitress or back in the textile mills, she's doing very well. She's been published in *Quest: A Feminist Quarterly, Off Our Backs,* and *Conditions.* She hasn't been published in half the places she intends to be.

Gloria Evangelina Anzaldúa, *b. 1946, a Chicana from South Texas.* Gloria Anzaldua has worked in the fields, taught Third World Women's Literature, cleaned houses. She coordinates El Mundo Surdo (The Left-Handed World), a feminist reading series in San Francisco, and is a member of Dial-a-Token, five Third World Women who give readings and workshops. She co-edited *This Bridge Called My Back: Writings by Radical Women of Color* with Cherríe Moraga (Persephone Press).

Sharon Barba, *b. 1943, Maumee, Ohio.* A small-town Ohio origin. Escaped from Ohio to New Mexico (my adopted/chosen home) in 1967. Having been bounced out of one teaching job for being an "uppity woman," I'm currently teaching remedial English. Publishing my lesbian poems is important to me because it affirms who I really am and what I really care about (poetry and women), *vs.* that straight-arrow English teacher.

Robin Becker, *b. 1951, Philadelphia.* Robin Becker teaches in The Writing Program at Massachusetts Institute of Technology. *Personal Effects,* a collection of work by three poets, includes a selection of her poems (Alice James Books, Cambridge, Mass.). Robin struggles to maintain a dual career as teacher/writer and is a frequent resident at art colonies including The

Ragdale Foundation (Lake Forest, Illinois), the Wurlitzer Foundation (New Mexico), and Cummington Community of the Arts (Cummington, Mass.).

Becky Birtha, *b. 1948, Hampton, Virginia.* I come from a Black middle-class background. Grew up primarily in Philadelphia (1953-1966). I'm currently in transition from a ten-year teaching (pre-school) career, to (hopefully) a lifestyle in which writing is more central. I write fiction and book reviews also. My work has appeared in many lesbian and/or feminist publications, most frequently in *Azalea* and *The Feminist Review.*

Bobbie Bishop, *b. 1944, Washington, D.C.* My daddy is from West Virginia, my mother from Nebraska. I have travelled across the country and lived in Puerto Rico. My life until last year was a terrifying journey. Now at 37, I hope to put all my trials in a clown suit. I work in an office and someday I will do theatre. I cherish myself, my daughter and the woman I love.

Ellen Marie Bissert, *b. 1947, Bay Ridge, Brooklyn.* Ellen Marie Bissert is the author of *the immaculate conception of the blessed virgin dyke* and editor of *13th Moon,* a literary magazine publishing women. "While I could not have written my work without the context of lesbian-feminism, my experience as a small press writer and editor has made me sensitive to the class bias in the women's press community."

Julie Blackwomon, *b. 1943, Saluda, Virginia.* At five my mother moved my brother and me to Philadelphia, where she supported us on domestic wages and later as a beautician. At 37 I still live in South Philly and support myself, my 14 year old daughter, and my art by working at a hard hat job in a refinery. I write because I have to, because I love the taste sound smell and feel of words.

Alice Bloch, *b. 1947, Youngstown, Ohio.* Alice Bloch came out as a lesbian in 1971 after a last-ditch attempt to become an Orthodox Jewish housewife in Israel. She now lives in Topanga, California, and is writing a novel, *Elisheva in the Promised Land,* based on the events of 1971. Her book *Lifetime Guarantee* will be published by Persephone Press in Spring 1981.

Karen Brodine, *b. 1947, Seattle.* Karen Brodine is a typesetter and teaches writing part-time. Her work has been published in feminist magazines such as *Conditions, Room, Wild Iris, The Second Wave, Heresies,* and *Hanging Loose.* Her third book of poetry, *Illegal Assembly,* was published in 1980 by Hanging Loose Press. She is a socialist feminist and is a member of the Women Writers Union, Radical Women, and The Freedom Socialist Party. She lives in San Francisco, and is working on a new book entitled *Woman Sitting At The Machine, Thinking.*

Olga Broumas, *b. 1949, Greece.* My mother was born in Alexandria, Egypt, the youngest of nine, to a handsome, almost albino in her paleness Greek emigrée from Andros, an Aegean island neighbor to Syros, which saw me born as my mother fled the internal war in the capital, Athens, where she followed my father, an orphan from Roumeli, who had, as a young officer, been wounded in North Africa, and been placed under her volunteer care.

Rita Mae Brown, *b. 1944, Hanover, Pennsylvania.* Grew up in York, Pennsylvania, and Ft. Lauderdale, Florida. Currently lives in Charlottesville, Virginia. An early lesbian activist, she helped found *The Furies* and has published many articles about theory and practice in the women's movement as well as two books of poetry, one book of essays and three novels. "York is only a few miles from the Mason-Dixon line, and my heart has *always* been on the south side of that border."

Wilmette Brown, *b. 1946, Newark, New Jersey.* Veteran of the civil rights movement, the anti-war movement, Black Studies, and the Black Panther Party; former history teacher in Zambia, Central Africa; Wilmette Brown is now executive director of Black Women for Wages for Housework (U.S.A.) and a spokeswoman for Wages Due Lesbians and the New York Prostitutes Collective, three organizations in the international Wages for Housework Campaign. She is most recently a successful fighter against cancer. You can reach her at: P.O. Box 830, Brooklyn, New York 11202.

Ruthe D. Canter, *b. 1950, Hartford, Connecticut.* I incite women workers to riot and boast supernatural communication with felines. Half my life is spent in supermarket checkout lines, the other half in quiet ecstasy with my lover and cats in San Francisco's Mission District. I have written locally for *Grassroots, Downtown Women's News,* taught at Area women's prisons and have authored some of the best lesbian graffiti.

Cheryl Clarke, *b. 1947, Washington, D.C.* Cheryl Clarke, a native of Washington, D.C., has lived and worked in New Brunswick, New Jersey, for 11 years. She has studied literature at Howard (1965-69) and Rutgers (1969-75) Universities. She believes poetry is and can be an instrument of struggle and liberation. Her poetic energy is fueled by her Black lesbian feminist identity. She is currently employed as a social worker in the field of community mental health and aging. She and her lover share work, a house, and parenting in Highland Park, New Jersey.

Jan Clausen, *b. 1950, North Bend, Oregon.* Jan Clausen grew up in the Pacific Northwest and now lives in Brooklyn; both trees and words claim her attention. She has published two collections of poetry and one of fiction. She edits *Conditions* magazine, does political organizing (most recently for the Women's Pentagon Action), and tries not to worry about money. She and her lover are raising a daughter.

Michelle Cliff, *b. 1946, Kingston, Jamaica.* Grew up in New York (Staten Island) and Jamaica. I am a Jamaican by birth and heritage, a woman of color, with both slaves and slaveholders in my background. I have spent the past few years on work which investigates my identity as a woman of color, a lesbian, and a feminist. I consider myself a historian.

Alison Colbert, *b. 1949, Washington, D.C.* Of Irish and Russian Jewish ancestry, she has lived most of the last decade in New York City. She has been a collective member of *Sojourner* magazine, the coordinator of the women's poetry reading series at the Focus II Coffeehouse, and an editor of *Women Writing.* Her first book of poems is *Let the Circle Be Unbroken* (1976).

Clare Coss, *b. 1935, New Brunswick, New Jersey.* Grew up in New Brunswick and New Orleans. Clare Coss is a playwright, poet and psychotherapist. She is co-author (with Sondra Segal and Roberta Sklar) of *The Daughters Cycle: Daughters, Sister/Sister, Electra Speaks,* produced at the Women's Interart Theatre, N.Y.C., 1977-1980. Her work has appeared in *Works, Aphra,* and *Chrysalis,* and been produced by The Berkshire Theatre Festival, The American Place Theatre, The Vancouver Women's Theatre.

Martha Courtot, *b. 1941, Cincinnati, Ohio.* Went to New York City at 19 to become a famous writer and be a lesbian. Had three daughters instead. Poetry as an essential subversive act. My roots: matriarchal hillbilly. My daughters continue to teach me while their futures depend on the work of radical feminism. As a Fat Woman, I struggle with the anti-fat oppression in heterosexual and lesbian culture. Published in many women's periodicals, including *Woman Spirit, Heresies, Lady-Unique, Primavera, Sinister Wisdom.* My new manuscript: *Night-River.*

Jane Creighton, *b. 1952, Williamsport, Pennsylvania.* I'm the former editor and publisher of the poetry magazine *Sailing the Road Clear* and have recently been working as an editor of Out & Out Books. I set type for a living and am at work right now on a journal and other material derived from a trip I made in 1977 through Iran, Afghanistan, and Pakistan. My first collection of poems is entitled *Ceres in an Open Field* (Out & Out, 1980).

Elsa Gidlow, *b. 1898, Hull, Yorkshire, England.* Family migrated to Montreal area of Canada when she was six hoping for improved financial condition. Up to age 15 lived in a poor French Canadian village with little schooling. Went to work at 16 in Montreal; moved alone to New York City at age 21. Learned editing. Later (1926), moved to San Francisco eventually to live as a free-lance journalist, always struggling.

Rebecca Gordon, *b. 1952, New York City.* Grew up: Washington, D.C. Rebecca Gordon hails from a broken Jewish-Gentile home. She has worked as a housepainter, liquor store clerk, ice cream cone packer, secretary, and feminist bookstore manager. Her poems have appeared in *Calyx, off our backs, Sinister Wisdom,* and *Conditions.* She is currently preparing a collection, *Hand Over Hand.*

Judy Grahn, *b. 1940, Chicago.* I am White and went to a Black college, I am Anglo and grew up in Mestizo Nuevo Mexico, I am Occidental and all my West Coast neighbors are of Asian descent, I was raised Protestant and the family to whom I am closest is Jewish, I have lived with few material possessions and have often felt fabulously wealthy, especially in love; and I identify with nearly everyone.

Susan Griffin, *b. 1943, Los Angeles.* Susan Griffin is a thirty-eight year old woman, a poet and a thinker, a lesbian and a feminist. She has lived in California all of her life, and in Berkeley for twenty years. She shares a home with another woman and their two daughters. She is fascinated with structures of the mind and kinds of knowledge, knowledge of the body, of feeling. She is currently at work on a play, and a collection of poetry. Her first book was published by Alta at the Shameless Hussy Press in 1971. She has just completed *Pornography and Silence* which will be published by Harper & Row in Spring, 1981.

Marilyn Hacker, *b. 1942, The Bronx.* Grew up: New York City. San Francisco 1967-70, London 1970-76. Marilyn Hacker is the author of *Taking Notice* (Knopf, 1980), *Separations* (Knopf, 1976), and *Presentation Piece* (Viking, 1974)—which received the National Book Award in poery in 1975. She is 38 years old, and lives in New York City with a seven-year-old Black Jewish Woman named Iva.

M.F.Hershman, *b. 1951, Cleveland, Ohio.* M.F.Hershman lives in Brookline, Massachusetts. She teaches college in the Boston area and reviews for *The Boston Globe.* She is active in Lesbian and Gay Media Advocates, a group working to change the coverage (and lack thereof) of lesbians and gay men in the media. Her poetry and fiction have appeared in places such as *The Beloit Poetry Journal, Ms. Magazine, Sojourner, Poetry-on-the-Buses, Seems,* and in translation in Dutch.

Teresa "Osa" Hidalgo-de la Riva, *b. 1954, Stockton, California.* At 26, Osa teaches at San Joaquin Delta College, conducts creative writing workshops in prisons, juvenile halls, and public school environments. Through Poetry-in-the-Schools Program she has been a poet-in-residence in East Los Angeles, San Francisco Mission District and the San Joaquin Valley. From a family of artistas, Osa began writing poetry at the age of eight. She co-founded a multi-cultural art center and school, CENTRO de ARTE, Long Beach, California, with her mother, Lola de la Riva. Osa received her M.A. in Creative Writing at San Francisco State University.

Frankie Hucklenbroich, *b. 1939, St.Louis.* Mother is Irish-Indian, father German and Polish; both, oldtime Catholics. I was their "devil," exorcised 23 years ago from that patriarchal, blue-collar, arid Midwest home. Since then—waitress, addict, college grad, businesswoman, factory-worker, barmaid, never and always learning—I've been one more maverick woman who writes from the bizarreté, the terror, joy, anger, fierceness—and humor—of anyone's survival.

Melanie Kaye, *b. 1945, Brooklyn.* melanie kaye is a jewish wildwoman poet born in brooklyn 1945. she spent the 70s in oregon teaching women's studies and organizing to stop violence against women, an obsession which has pursued her to sante fe where she now lives, and which is reflected (along with obsessions about the holocaust, resistance, sex, loving women, hard times, etc.) in her book *We Speak in Code* (Motheroot 1980).

Willyce Kim, *b. 1946, Honolulu, Hawaii.* Revitalized and experiencing numerous visions in my 35th year. Still living in California. Still struggling for loose change. As handsome as ever. Wish you were here.

Irena Klepfisz, *b. 1941, Warsaw, Poland.* Jewish. Came to New York City: 1949. Worked through college and graduate school as baby-sitter, pianist, typist, receptionist, library assistant, insurance claims adjuster, medical transcriber. Since 1969, taught English, Yiddish, Women's Studies, women's poetry workshops. Also worked as editor, Yiddish translator, proofreader, typist, legal secretary. Poet: *Periods of Stress* (Piecework Press). Founder/ editor: *Conditions*. N.Y.S. CAPS poetry grant: 1976. No children. Three cats. Plants.

Ana Kowalkowska, *b. 1948, Vallejo, California.* Ana Kowalkowska lives in California's Napa Valley and has been writing bilingual poetry since 1970. Three of her poems were included in a dramatic presentation performed by local women. She is currently writing short stories.

Jacqueline Lapidus, *b. 1941, New York City.* Grew up: New York City. Jacqueline Lapidus taught English in Greece for three years before settling in Paris where she has now lived for the past 14 years. She teaches and does translations for a living, but writing poems is her real work; she is also active in feminist groups and campaigns, travels whenever she can, and has given readings in the U.S.

Eleanor Lerman, *b. 1952, New York City.* I was born and raised in New York City and spent a few years in Far Rockaway where my main activity was trying to find somebody with a car to drive me into Manhattan. Since I now live in Manhattan and can afford my own transportation I suppose my life can be seen, in some small ways, as a success.

Audre Lorde, *b. 1934, New York City.* Black, feminist, mother. Professor at John Jay College of Criminal Justice. Latest book is *The Cancer Journals*, published by Spinsters, Ink.

Judith McDaniel, *b. 1943, San Antonio, Texas.* Born on an Air Force base; attended 21 schools before 12th grade. Judith McDaniel is a writer and teacher who lives in an old farmhouse in very rural upstate New York. With Maureen Brady, she operates the feminist publishing company Spinsters, Ink. Her poems and reviews have appeared in *Conditions, Sinister Wisdom,* and other lesbian and feminist journals.

Jean Mollison, *b. 1918, Brooklyn.* Jean Mollison has renovated a farmhouse in upstate New York where she has lived for over 35 years, and where she pursues her ongoing interests in carpentry, masonry, and gardening. Although she has written many poems and submitted for publication during the Forties and Fifties, this is her first published work.

Honor Moore, *b. 1945, New York City.* Grew up: New York, Jersey City, Indianapolis, D.C. Though I write in other forms, poetry is the means of the vision. *Mourning Pictures,* a verse play about my mother's death, was produced on Broadway (1974) and published in *The New Women's Theatre: Ten Plays by Contemporary American Women* (Vintage, 1977). I am completing a first book of poems and beginning a life of my artist grandmother, Margarett Sargent McKean.

Cherríe Moraga, *b. 1952, Los Angeles.* Cherríe Moraga is a Chicana feminist and co-editor of *This Bridge Called My Back: Writings by Radical Women of Color* (Persephone). She is a first-generation writer and writes to remember that. The poems included in *Lesbian Poetry: An Anthology* are part of a manuscript entitled *Loving in the War Years.*

Felice Newman, *b. 1956, New York City.* Felice Newman edited *Cameos: 12 Small Press Women Poets* (The Crossing Press, 1978). Her poetry has appeared in *The Little Magazine, Sinister Wisdom,* and other magazines. She is an editor of Cleis Press, a feminist publishing company.

Barbara Noda, *b. 1953, California.* Barbara Noda is a writer of Japanese ancestry. She grew up in the Salinas Valley in California. Her first book of poetry, *Strawberries,* is published by Shameless Hussy Press. She has written a play titled *Aw Shucks (Shikata Ga Nai)* and is currently working on a novel.

Pat Parker, *b. 1944, Houston, Texas.* Pat Parker is a Black Lesbian Feminist writer who has been working and living in the Bay Area for the last 17 years. She has published four books of poetry and her work can be heard on four albums. She has read her work throughout the U. S. and Europe.

Minnie Bruce Pratt, *b. 1946, Alabama.* Grew up: Alabama. Minnie Bruce Pratt is a collective editor of *Feminary: A Feminist Journal for the South.* which emphasizes the lesbian vision and is committed to an examination of racial issues. Her prose has appeared in *The Coming Out Stories* and *Top Ranking.* Her memoir-essay on "Rebellion" appeared in *Feminary.*

Adrienne Rich, *b. 1929, Baltimore.* Graduated Radcliffe College. Married 1953, left marriage 1970. Have three sons. Through 1960's, involved in civil rights and anti-war movements, feminist movement since 1970. Have taught basic writing, poetry workshops, women's studies at various universities. Besides poetry, two prose books: *Of Woman Born: Motherhood as Experience and Institution* (1976) and *On Lies, Secrets and Silence* (1979). Living since 1976 with the writer Michelle Cliff; since 1979 in western Massachusetts, where we co-edit the lesbian-feminist journal *Sinister Wisdom.*

Sapphire, *b. California.* I am a Black woman writer living in New York.

May Sarton, *b. 1912, Wondelgem, Belgium.* Daughter of George Sarton, historian of science, and Mabel Elwes Sarton, English artist. Refugees in World War I, settled finally in Cambridge, Massachusetts. Joined Eva Le Gallienne's Civic Repertory Theatre; directed The Apprentice Group. Founded The Apprentice Theatre; turned her back on the theatre when it closed (1935). Published 13 books of poems, 15 novels, three books of memoirs and three journals, the last, *Recovering.* Lives in York, Maine.

Susan Saxe, *b. 1949, Hartford, Connecticut.* Grew up: Albany, New York (1950-66). Susan Saxe is a Lesbian feminist and a political prisoner. She wrote "Notes" while a fugitive for armed anti-war actions in 1970. Jailed since 1975, this nice Jewish girl has made it past 30 still an activist, a poet and an up-front dyke. She aspires someday to become an old battleaxe as well.

Martha Shelley, *b. 1943, New York City.* I was born in Brooklyn, to a working-class Jewish family. For many years, I enjoyed gay spinsterhood, and a glorious career in politics and communications: Radicalesbians, Gay Liberation Front, RAT newspaper, WBAI-FM (producer of lesbian-feminist shows), and the Women's Press Collective. Now I'm living with a lover and three kids, and looking for a good-paying job.

Susan Sherman, *b. 1939, Philadelphia.* Grew up: Los Angeles. Susan Sherman was editor of IKON, a radical culture magazine; a delegate to the Dialectics of Liberation conference in London in 1967; and a delegate to the Cuban Cultural Congress in Havana in 1968. Her poetry has been published in many magazines and anthologies including *Poetry, The Nation, El Corno Emplumado, Conditions, 13th Moon.* She currently lives and works in New York City. Her two available books of poetry are *With Anger/With Love, Women Poems Love Poems.*

Esther Silverman, *b. 1948, Cuba.* Grew up: Cuba and New York City. Esther Silverman has been living in New York since 1961. Raised by East European Jewish parents in a Hispanic environment, she has assimilated both cultures. She identifies strongly with these two seemingly divergent backgrounds. Interwoven into her work is her profound love for women.

Rota Silverstrini, *b. 1941, the South Bronx.* I was brought up in the South Bronx. I've been out all my life; writing since the age of eight. Currently, I make my home in the Bronx with my twin and her three children; we're very close. I'm writing an autobiographical novel; also working in pottery, acrylics, gouache, and pen and ink.

Barbara Smith, *b. 1946, Cleveland, Ohio.* I was raised by a family of transplanted Southern women. I have been doing Black feminist organizing since 1973. I didn't start writing seriously until I came out in 1975. I support myself by teaching women's studies at the University of Massachusetts in Boston. My work has appeared in various publications including

Conditions, Chrysalis and *Freedomways.* I dream of writing full time, making a film about Third World feminism and living long enough to see a radical increase of freedom for those of us who need it. I co-edited *Conditions: Five, The Black Women's Issue.*

Wendy Stevens, *b. 1953, New York City.* I write short fiction, non-fiction and poetry and have been a member of the *off our backs* collective for six years. At present, I am earning my living writing children's educational films and writing a book on "young women and the juvenile justice system." I share my living space with a young woman who is my foster child. Lately, I have been putting a lot of my energy into child advocacy and young people's rights.

Lynn Strongin, *b. 1939, New York City.* I was raised in New York City where I pursued early studies in musical composition. Began writing poetry in college, and publishing in California in the sixties where I became involved in the Feminist movement. Am currently completing a three-year labor, *Emma's Book,* the novel I've written on a woman doctor.

Lorraine Sutton, *b. 1949, Caguas, Puerto Rico.* Raised in Manhattan and lived for many years in the Bronx. She has published in *El Tiempo, Latin New York, Sunbury,* and *West End. SAYcred LAYdy* (1975) was her first book of poems. For the past several years, she has been living and working in the Cleveland area.

Kitty Tsui, *b. 1952, Hong Kong.* Grew up: England and Hong Kong.
I claim language as my own tongue–
the bittermelon taste of Chinese, English,
the crunch, crisp as snow pears, English, Chinese,
embroidering the links between
history, now, and that-to-come;
my grandmother/sister
and my mother, the earth.

Wendy Brooks Wieber, *b. 1951, New Rochelle, New York.* I now live in California where my partner and I are renovating an old farmhouse and raising Morgan horses. Here natural imagery has become more central to my poetry, reflecting my own celebration of feminine spirit.

Fran Winant, *b. 1943, New York City.* I was born in Brooklyn, lower middle class, Jewish; worked as a photo researcher, cab driver, word processor. I have written three books of poetry available from Violet Press. Sustaining a small press has been a devastating experience. Spirituality, the healing/sharing aspect of the women's community, strongly influences my current writing.

Susan Wood-Thompson, *b. 1942, Dallas.* Has lived: New Mexico, Virginia, South Carolina, Washington, D.C. My work experience includes nursing aide, reader to blind people, college instructor, poet in the schools, and currently, teacher of poetry-writing workshops for women. *Atalanta*, *Feminary*, and *Sinister Wisdom* have published my poetry. I participate in the Woman Writes Conferences for Southern lesbians. Working with six women from the South, I published a book of my poems, *Crazy Quilt*.

Elise Young, *b. 1946, Cambridge, Massachusetts.* I am 35 years old, of Jewish ancestry, twin and sister, dedicated to revisioning language and reclaiming our healing powers, through writing, teaching, meditating, conversing. I live in the country where I'm learning skills that are releasing me from the numbing effects of male civilization. Poems have appeared in *Quest*, *Colloquy*, *Ms.*, *13th Moon*, *Aphra* and *Amazon Poetry*.

Work by Contributors

The following is a list of currently available poetry and other books by contributors, anthologies they have compiled, feminist journals they edit, and recordings of their work. Addresses are included for all lesbian, feminist, and other "small" presses; if a press has published the work of more than one contributor, the address is included under a separate heading at the end of this listing. Most of this work is available in feminist bookstores; all of it can be ordered directly from the presses or distributors. All books are paperbacks unless otherwise indicated.

The price information that follows each entry does not include a charge for postage and handling; while these rates differ slightly from press to press, most costs would be met by your including 85 cents postage/handling for each book (or record) you order. If you live in the same state as the press from which you are ordering, you should also include any applicable state sales tax. While large commercial presses have the resources to bill you, women's presses do not—so help them out by prepaying (in U.S. currency).

POETRY BOOKS

Paula Gunn Allen, *Coyote's Daylight Trip* (La Confluencia, P.O. Box 409, Albuquerque, NM 87108), 1978, 50 pp., $3.95. *The Blind Lion* (Thorp Springs Press), 1975, $2.00.

Robin Becker [Helena Minton, Marilyn Zuckerman], *Personal Effects* (Alice James Books, 138 Mt.Auburn St., Cambridge, MA 02138), 1977, 86 pp., $3.50.

Ellen Marie Bissert, *the immaculate conception of the blessed virgin dyke* (13th Moon, Drawer F, Inwood Station, New York, NY 10034), 1977, 64 pp., $3.00.

Karen Brodine, *Illegal Assembly* (Hanging Loose Press), 1980, 63 pp., $3.00.

Olga Broumas, *Soie Sauvage* (Copper Canyon Press, Box 371), Port Townsend, WA 98368), 1979, 47 pp., $4.00. *Caritas* (Jackrabbit Press, RD 1, Box 313A, Plainfield, VT 05667), 1976, 12 pp., $2.50. *Beginning with O* (Yale University Press), 1977, 74 pp., $2.95.

Rita Mae Brown, *The Hand That Cradles the Rock* (published Diana Press; distributed The Crossing Press), 1974, 80 pp., $4.50. *Songs to a Handsome Woman* (published Diana Press; distributed The Crossing Press), 1973, 70 pp., $4.50.

Jan Clausen, *Waking at the Bottom of the Dark* (Long Haul Press, Box 592, Van Brunt Station, Brooklyn, NY 11215), 1979, 78 pp., $3.00. *After Touch* (published Out & Out Books; distributed Long Haul Press), 1975, 80 pp., $2.00.

Michelle Cliff, *Claiming an Identity They Taught Me To Despise* (Persephone Press), 1980, 72 pp., $4.00.

Alison Colbert, *Let the Circle Be Unbroken* (Women Writing Press, P.O. Box 1035, Cathedral Station, New York, NY 10025), 1976, 64 pp., $2.75.

Martha Courtot, *Journey* (Pearlchild, 2800 St.Paul No.259, Santa Rosa, CA 95405), 1977, 22 pp., $2.00. *Tribe* (Pearlchild), 1977, 28 pp., $2.50.

Jane Creighton, *Ceres in an Open Field* (Out & Out Books), 1980, 72 pp., $3.50.

Elsa Gidlow, *Makings for Meditation* (Druid Heights Books, 685 Camino del Canyon, Muir Woods, Mill Valley, CA 94941), 1973, 48 pp., $2.00.

Judy Grahn, *The Work of a Common Woman: The Collected Poetry of Judy Grahn, 1964-1977*; Introduction by Adrienne Rich (Diana Press—out of print; reprinted St. Martin's Press), 1978, 158 pp., $8.95 (hardcover). *She Who* (published Diana Press; distributed The Crossing Press), 1977, 89 pp., $6.00. *A Woman Is Talking to Death* (published Women's Press Collective; distributed The Crossing Press), 1974, 19 pp., $2.50. *Edward the Dyke and Other Poems* (published Women's Press Collective; distributed The Crossing Press), 1971, 66 pp., $2.50.

Susan Griffin, *Like the Iris of an Eye* (Harper & Row), 1976, 134 pp., $4.95.

Marilyn Hacker, *Taking Notice* (Knopf), 1980, 121 pp., $5.95. "Taking Notice," sonnet sequence (Out & Out Books), 1980, $2.00. *Separations* (Knopf), 1976, 109 pp., $3.95. *Presentation Piece* (Viking), 1974, 116 pp., $2.95.

Melanie Kaye, *We Speak in Code* (Motheroot, 214 Dewey St., Pittsburgh, PA 15218), 1980, 108 pp., $4.75.

Willyce Kim, *Under the Rolling Sky* (Maud Gonne Press), 1976, 39 pp., $2.50. *Eating Artichokes* (Women's Press Collective), 1972, n.p., $2.00. Order both from Kim, 1647 Edith St., Berkeley, CA 94703.

Irena Klepfisz, *periods of stress* (published Out & Out Books; distributed Piecework Press, GPO Box 2422, Brooklyn, NY 11202), 1975, 61 pp., $2.00.

Jacqueline Lapidus, *Starting Over* (Out & Out Books), 1977, 63 pp., $3.50. *Ready to Survive* (Hanging Loose Press), 1975, 63 pp., $3.00.

Joan Larkin, *Housework* (Out & Out Books), 1975, 80 pp., $3.50.

Eleanor Lerman, *Come the Sweet By and By* (University of Massachusetts Press), 1975, 73 pp., $3.50. *Armed Love* (Wesleyan University Press), 1973, 64 pp., $3.45.

Audre Lorde, *The Black Unicorn* (Norton), 1978, 122 pp., $3.95. *Coal* (Norton), 1976, 70 pp., $2.95. *New York Head Shop and Museum* (Broadside Press, 12651 Old Mill Place, Detroit, MI 48238), 1974, 68 pp., $3.50.

Honor Moore, *Poem in Four Movements for My Sister Marion* (Out & Out Books), 1980, $1.00. *Polemic No. 1* (c/o Wendy Weil, Julian Bach Literary Agency, 747 Third Ave., New York, NY 10017), $1.50 includes postage.

Barbara Noda, *Strawberries* (Shameless Hussy Press, Box 3092, Berkeley, CA), 1980.

Pat Parker, *Movement in Black: The Collected Poetry of Pat Parker, 1961-1978* (published Diana Press; distributed The Crossing Press), 1978, 157 pp., $8.75 (hardcover). *Womanslaughter and Other Poems* (published Diana Press; distributed The Crossing Press), 1978, 63 pp., $3.00. *Child of Myself* (published Shameless Hussy Press, Women's Press Collective; distributed The Crossing Press), 1972, 1975, 1977, n.p., $3.00.

Adrienne Rich, *The Dream of a Common Language* (Norton), 1978, 77 pp., $2.95. *Poems: Selected and New, 1950-1974* (Norton), 1975, 256 pp., $4.50. *Diving into the Wreck* (Norton), 1973, 62 pp., $1.95. *The Will to Change* (Norton), 1971, 67 pp., $1.95. *Leaflets* (Norton), 1969, 71 pp., $4.95. *Necessities of Life* (Norton), 1966, 79 pp., $1.95. *Snapshots of a Daughter-in-Law* (Norton), 1963, 64 pp., $2.95.

May Sarton, *Halfway to Silence* (Norton), 1980, 64 pp., $4.95. *Selected Poems*, eds. Serena Sue Hilsinger and Lois Brynes (Norton), 1978, 206 pp., $3.45. *A Private Mythology* (Norton), 1966, 107 pp., $4.00. *Collected Poems, 1930-1973* (Norton), 1974, 416 pp., $10.00 (hardcover). *A Grain of Mustard Seed* (Norton), 1971, $2.95.

Susan Saxe, *Talk Among the Womenfolk* (published Common Woman Press; distributed Susan Saxe Defense Committee, Box 39, West Somerville, MA 02144), 1976.

Martha Shelley, *Crossing the DMZ* (published Women's Press Collective; distributed Bay Area Samizdat, 542 25th St., No.335, Oakland, CA 94612), 1974, 53 pp., $2.50. *Lovers and Mothers* (Bay Area Samizdat), 1981.

Susan Sherman, *Women Poems Love Poems* (distributed Out & Out Books), 1975, 27 pp., $2.00. *With Anger/With Love, Selections: Poems and Prose, 1963-1973* (published Mulch Press; distributed Out & Out Books), 1974, 69 pp., $3.50.

Lynn Strongin, *Countrywoman/Surgeon* (L'Epervier Press, 726 Hayes, Seattle, WA 98109), 1979, 70 pp., $6.95 (hardcover). *Nightmare of Mouse* (L'Epervier Press), 1977, 82 pp. *Toccata of the Disturbed Child* (Fallen Angel Press, 1913 West McNichols, C6, Highland Park, MI 48203), 1977, 34 pp., $2.00. *A Hacksaw Brightness* (Ironwood Press, P.O. Box 40907, Tucson, AZ 85717), 1977, $2.50. *Paschal Poem: Now in the Green Year's Turning* (Sun Ring Press), 1976. *Shrift: A Winter Sequence* (Thorp Springs Press), 1975, $2.00. *The Dwarf Cycle* (Thorp Springs Press), 1972, n.p., $2.50.

Lorraine Sutton, *SAYcred LAYdy* (Sunbury Press, Box 274, Jerome Ave. Station, Bronx, NY 10468), 1975, 32 pp., $2.75.

Fran Winant, *Goddess of Lesbian Dreams* (Violet Press), 1980, 63 pp., $3.50. *Dyke Jacket* (Violet Press), 1976, 64 pp., $3.00. *Looking at Women* (Violet Press), 1971, 34 pp., $1.00.

Susan Wood-Thompson, *Crazy Quilt* (published Crone Books; distributed The Crossing Press), 1980, 61 pp., $3.00 (also available on cassette).

Elise Young, *Medusa's Hair: Poetry of Lesbian Re-Envisioning* (Mountainwind Products, Box 92, Middlefield, MA 01243), 1980, 17 pp., $4.00.

OTHER WRITINGS

Alice Bloch, *Lifetime Guarantee*, novel (Persephone Press), 1981.

Rita Mae Brown, *Six of One*, novel (Harper & Row), 1978, 336 pp., $2.50. *A Plain Brown Rapper*, essays (published Diana Press; distributed The Crossing Press), 1976, 236 pp., $6.95. *In Her Day*, novel (Daughters, Inc., MS 590, P. O. Box 42999, Houston, TX 77042), 1976, 196 pp., $4.50. *Rubyfruit Jungle*, novel (Harper & Row), 1973, 246 pp., $2.50.

Wilmette Brown [and Margaret Prescod-Roberts, Norma Steele], *Black Women: Bringing It All Back Home*, essays (Falling Wall Press; distributed Publication Distribution Services, 175 Fifth Ave., Suite 814, New York, NY), 1980, 48 pp., $2.95.

Elly Bulkin, *Racism and Writing: Some Implications for White Lesbian Critics*, reprinted from *Sinister Wisdom 13* (Lesbian-Feminist Study Clearinghouse), 1980, 11 pp., $.90. *An Interview with Adrienne Rich*, reprinted from *Conditions: One* and *Two* (Lesbian-Feminist Study Clearinghouse), 1977, 30 pp., $1.30.

Jan Clausen, *Mother Sister Daughter Lover*, stories (The Crossing Press), 1980, 136 pp., $4.95.

Susan Griffin, *Pornography and Silence: Culture's Revenge Against Nature* (Harper & Row), 1981. *Rape: The Power of Consciousness* (Harper & Row), 1979, 134 pp., $3.95. *Women and Nature: The Roaring Inside Her* (Harper & Row), 1978, 263 pp., $3.95.

Audre Lorde, *The Cancer Journals* (Spinsters, Ink), 1980, 79 pp., $4.00. *Man Child: A Black Lesbian Feminist's Response*, reprinted from *Conditions: Four* (Lesbian-Feminist Study Clearinghouse), 1979, 4 pp., $.35. *Uses of the Erotic: The Erotic as Power,* reprinted from *Chrysalis No. 9* (Out & Out Books), 1978, $1.00. *Scratching the Surface: Some Notes on Barriers to Women and Loving,* reprinted from *The Black Scholar* (Lesbian-Feminist Study Clearinghouse), 1978, 5 pp., $.40.

Judith McDaniel, *Reconstituting the World: The Poetry and Vision of Adrienne Rich* (Spinsters, Ink), 1978, 24 pp., $1.50.

Barbara Noda, Kitty Tsui [and Z. Wong], *Coming Out: We Are Here in the Asian Community: A Dialogue with Three Asian Women*, reprinted from *Bridge: An Asian American Perspective* (Lesbian-Feminist Study Clearinghouse), 1979, 3 pp., $.25.

Adrienne Rich, *On Lies, Secrets and Silence: Selected Prose, 1966-1978* (Norton), 1979, 310 pp., $3.95. *Of Woman Born: Motherhood as Experience and Institution* (Norton), 1976, 318 pp., $2.95. *The Meaning of Our Love for Women Is What We Have Constantly to Expand*, pamphlet (Out & Out Books), 1977, $1.00.

May Sarton, *Recovering: A Journal* (Norton), 1980, 246 pp., $12.95 (hardcover). *A Reckoning,* novel (Norton), 1978, 254 pp., $9.95 (hardcover). *Mrs. Stevens Hears the Mermaids Singing,* novel (Norton), 1974, 220 pp., $3.95. Thirteen other novels, two other journals, and three books of memoirs.

Barbara Smith [and Beverly Smith], *"I Am Not Meant to Be Alone and Without You Who Understand": Letters from Black Feminists, 1972-1978,* reprinted from *Conditions: Four* (Lesbian Feminist Study Clearinghouse), 1979, 8 pp., $.65.

Barbara Smith, *Toward a Black Feminist Criticism*, reprinted from *Conditions: Two* (Lesbian Feminist Study Clearinghouse), 1977, 20 pp., $.90; (Out & Out Books), 1980, $1.00.

Lynn Strongin, *Bones and Kim*, novel (Spinsters, Ink), 1980, 120 pp., $5.50.

POETRY ANTHOLOGIES EDITED

Sharon Barba [with Laura Chester], *Rising Tides: 20th Century American Women Poets* (Washington Square Press), 1973, 410 pp., $1.95.

Karen Brodine, *Hair-Raising* (Kelsey St. Press, 2824 Kelsey St., Berkeley, CA 94705), 1976, 48 pp., $3.75.

Felice Newman, *Cameos: 12 Small Press Poets* (The Crossing Press), 1978, 167 pp., $4.95.

Kitty Tsui [with Canyon, Nancy Hom, Genny Lim, Nellie Wong, Merle Woo], *Unbound Feet* (Isthmus Poetry Foundation, P. O. Box 6877, San Francisco, CA 94101), 1981.

Fran Winant, *We Are All Lesbians* (Violet Press), 1973, 64 pp., $2.00.

OTHER ANTHOLOGIES EDITED

Elly Bulkin, *Lesbian Fiction: An Anthology* (Persephone Press), 1981.

Judy Grahn, *True to Life Adventure Stories*, fiction (published Diana Press; distributed The Crossing Press), 1978, 224 pp., $5.00.

Honor Moore, *The New Women's Theatre: Ten Plays by Contemporary American Women* (Vintage/Random House), 1977, 537 pp., $5.95.

Cherríe Moraga and Gloria Anzaldúa, *This Bridge Called My Back: Writings by Radical Women of Color* (Persephone Press), 1981.

Barbara Smith [with Gloria T. Hull and Patricia Bell Scott], *Black Women's Studies* (The Feminist Press, Box 334, Old Westbury, NY 11568), 1981.

FEMINIST JOURNALS EDITED

Conditions, A Magazine of Writing by Women with an Emphasis on Writing by Lesbians. P. O. Box 56, Van Brunt Station, Brooklyn, NY 11215. $11/3 issues; $6 "hardship" subscription/3 issues. $22/institutional subscription. $4.50/single issue; $8/single issue to institutions. Free to women in prisons and mental institutions. Elly Bulkin and Jan Clausen, members of editorial collective; Irena Klepfisz, founding editor (1976-1980). *Conditions: Five, The Black Women's Issue*, Barbara Smith, co-editor.

Feminary, A Feminist Journal for the South Emphasizing the Lesbian Vision. P. O. Box 954, Chapel Hill, NC 27514. Individual subscriptions, $6.50/3 issues; institutions, $13.00/3 issues. Free to women in prisons and mental institutions. Minnie Bruce Pratt, member of editorial collective.

Sinister Wisdom, A Journal of Words and Pictures for the Lesbian Imagination in All Woman. P. O. Box 660, Amherst, MA 01004. Individual subscriptions (U. S. and Canada), $10/4 issues; $18/8 issues. Institutional subscriptions, $15/4 issues. Overseas subscriptions, $12/4 issues; $21/8 issues. $3 single issue; $4.50 single issue to institutions. Free to women in prisons and mental institutions. Michelle Cliff and Adrienne Rich, editors.

13th Moon, A Feminist Literary Magazine. Drawer F, Inwood Station, New York, NY 10034. Single issues $2.25 plus $.60 postage. Prices are double to institutions which require billing. Ellen Marie Bissert, editor.

RECORDINGS

Adrienne Rich Reading at Stanford (Stanford Program for Recordings in Sound), 1978.

The Poetry and Voice of Marilyn Hacker (Caedmon), 1975, $8.98.

A Sign/I Was Not Alone: A Poetry Reading, Joan Larkin, Audre Lorde, Honor Moore, Adrienne Rich (Out & Out Books), 1978, $6.00.

Where Would I Be Without You: The Poetry of Pat Parker and Judy Grahn (Olivia Records, P. O. Box 70237, Los Angeles, CA 90070), 1976, $5.50.

PRESS ADDRESSES

The Crossing Press, Trumansburg, NY 14886

Hanging Loose Press, 231 Wyckoff St., Brooklyn, NY 11217

Lesbian Feminist Study Clearinghouse, Women's Studies Program, 1012 CL, University of Pittsburgh, Pittsburgh, PA 15260 (minimum orders: $3.00)

Out & Out Books, 476 Second St., Brooklyn, NY 11215

Persephone Press, Inc., P.O. Box 7222, Watertown, MA 02172

Spinsters, Ink, RD 1 Argyle, NY 12809

Thorp Springs Press, 2311-C Woolsey, Berkeley, CA 94705

Violet Press, P. O. Box 398, New York, NY 10009

Some Additional Resources

The following is a list of selected articles about contemporary lesbian poetry and of interviews with and autobiographical statements by contributors. We have included here only work not already listed in the Notes to the "Introduction" and to "Lesbian Poetry in the Classroom" and in the Work by Contributors section. Reviews of books by contributors can be found in past and current issues of feminist journals and newspapers.

June S. Bakerman. "Work Is My Rest: A Conversation with May Sarton," *Moving Out*, Vol. 77, No. 1 and Vol. 7, No. 2 (1979), 8-12, 87. $1.75 from 4866 Third & Warren, Detroit, MI 48202.

Elly Bulkin. "The Places We Have Been: The Poetry of Susan Griffin," *Margins*, No. 23 (1975), pp. 31-34. $1.00 from P. O. Box A, Fair Water, WI 53931.

Jan Clausen. "The Question That Is Our Lives: The Poetry of Susan Sherman," *Conditions: One* (1977), pp. 66-76.

Anita Cornwell, " 'So Who's Giving Guarantees?': An Interview with Audre Lorde," *Sinister Wisdom 4* (1977), pp. 15-21.

Elsa Gidlow. "Memoirs," *Feminist Studies*, Vol. 6, No. 1 (Spring 1980), 103-127. $5.00 from Women's Studies Program, University of Maryland, College Park, MD 20742. "Glimpses of Glory," *Lady-Unique-Inclination-of-the-Night*, Cycle 5 (Autumn 1980), pp. 15-19. $3.50 from P. O. Box 803, New Brunswick, NJ 08903.

Susan Griffin. "Thoughts on Writing: A Diary," *The Writer and Her Work: Contemporary Women Writers Reflect on Their Art and Situation*, ed. Janet Sternburg (New York: Norton, 1980), pp. 107-120. $14.95 (hardcover).

Dori Hale. "An Interview with Honor Moore," *Sojourner* (April 1979). $.75 from 143 Albany St., Cambridge, MA 02139.

Robin Kaplan and Shelley Neiderbach. "An Interview with May Sarton," *Motheroot Journal*, Vol. 1, No. 4 (Fall/Winter 1979), 1, 10-11. $1.00 from 214 Dewey St., Pittsburgh, PA 15218.

Lynda Koolish. "The Incendiary Feminism of Lesbian Poetry," *San Francisco Bay Guardian* (March 23, 1978), p. 11. *A Whole New Poetry Beginning Here*, unpublished dissertation, University Microfilm, University of Michigan.

Judith McDaniel. "A Conversation with Olga Broumas," *New Women's Times Feminist Review*, No. 6 (August 31-September 13, 1979), pp. 16-17. $3.00 from 804 Meigs Street, Rochester, NY 14620. "An Interview with Jan Clausen," *Motheroot Journal* (Summer 1979), p. 2. "Interview with Michelle Cliff," *New Women's Times Feminist Review*, No. 15 (April/May 1981), pp. 11-14.

Inez Martinez. "The Poetry of Judy Grahn," *Margins*, No. 23 (1975), pp. 48-50.

Honor Moore. "My Grandmother Who Painted," *The Writer and Her Work*, pp. 45-70.

Minnie Bruce Pratt. "Rebellion," *Feminary*, Vol. XI, No. 1 and 2 (Fall 1980).

Adrienne Rich. "An Interview with Audre Lorde," *Woman Poet—The East* (Winter 1980-1981). Women in Literature, P. O. Box 12668, Reno, NV 89510.